The Confident Speaker

The
Confident
Speaker

How to Master Fear and Persuade an Audience

Ray Harlan

McGuinn & McGuire
PUBLISHING
Bradenton, Florida

Publisher's Cataloging-in-Publication Data

Harlan, Raymond C.
    The Confident Speaker.
    Includes index.
    1. Public speaking. 2. Oral communication.
I. Harlan, Raymond C. 1943- II. Title
PN4121.H37   1993   808.5'1   92-62046
ISBN 1-881117-01-4

Library of Congress Catalog Card Number: 92-62046

Printed in the United States of America

Dedicated to
my mother and father.

Acknowledgments

The writing of this book owes something to all the good teachers I have had, all the communication books I have read, all the successful speakers I have observed, and all the colleagues who have shared their insights with me. Since that list is quite long, I prefer to mention four sources which stand out from the others.

The basic idea for the book came while I was teaching the Briefing Preparation and Presentation Course at the Air Force Institute of Technology (AFIT). I am indebted to AFIT's Bob Weaver and his fellow syllabus writers for the kernels from which several of the following chapters have grown. The sections on organization, handling questions, and types of charts had their origin in that syllabus.

My father, Ross Harlan, read an early draft and suggested a number of additions. In a sense, his contributions started even earlier, since his conviction that communication skills were required for success and his own accomplishments as a speaker were major factors in my decision to study communication.

The recommendations of Christopher Carroll, Managing Editor at McGuinn & McGuire, proved invaluable, both in the overall organization of the book and in the structure of certain chapters. His close attention has made a much stronger book.

The contributions of my wife, Linda, have been less obvious, but equally important. Her buoyant spirit and calming influence have kept me on course through another major project.

Thanks.

Ray Harlan

Contents

Special Situations

Appendices

Introduction

This book can help you confront and conquer a fear worse than death. According to *The Book of Lists*, the one thing Americans fear most is speaking before a group.[1] The fear of death only rated number six on the list. (I wonder what would have happened if they had asked about the fear of death while speaking?) Unfortunately, speaking is not only scary, it is crucial to success. When 250 of the Fortune 500 firms were polled on the characteristics which made a college graduate a desirable job candidate, "speaking well" led the list.[2]

That presents ambitious managers and executives with a dilemma: the thing they fear the most is the one skill they can't succeed without!

In my speech workshops, I normally get a number of participants who have risen rapidly in their organizations by virtue of technical competence or managerial expertise. They have now arrived at a level where they must give regular presentations of some sort, which brings on the familiar *fear worse than death*. They feel trapped, knowing they will never get another promotion unless they learn to speak well.

A number of these very competent adults have told me they don't think they have what it takes to give a good speech. What it takes, however, in terms of physical abilities, is very slight. A speaker must be able to stand up, look at the audience, talk out loud, switch a projector on and off, and smile. All of which is well within the range of a normal adult. What blocks them, of course, is uncontrolled anxiety. Instead of mastering fear and anxiety, they are slaves to their own emotions.

This book offers a way out of the dilemma. Thousands of people have discovered how to cope with fear, harnessing their anxiety to make a speech or presentation better. The process is not especially mysterious. Successful orators have followed the same techniques ever since Aristotle described them over 2300 years ago. Whether you are briefing a six-person staff in your company's conference room, addressing hundreds at a professional luncheon, or talking with thousands via television, the basic tasks are the same:

> Analyze the situation.
>
> Organize your material.
>
> Rehearse effectively.
>
> Give your speech as rehearsed.
>
> Respond to your audience.

This book covers each point thoroughly. By mastering your anxiety and carefully following the steps in the speech-making process, you can develop the skills to give a confident and successful speech, whatever the occasion.

Most of this book's examples are drawn from typical speaking situations encountered by executives and managers in business, industry, and government, but the principles apply equally well to presentations in other fields, such as education, religion, and community service. Students and others aspiring to management jobs can use this book to master the art of speaking before it is demanded of them.

Anyone whose schedule is too tight to allow reading the entire book before the next speech can get the basic concepts by reading the executive summaries at the end of each chapter and then returning to those topics which are most pertinent. A manager with strong presentation skills can skim the summaries and pick out chapters which can help a struggling subordinate.

No one need continue to be miserable when faced with the need to speak. The concepts in this book, coupled with persistence, will enable anyone to master the art of persuasion. Remember, every good speaker you hear began as a bad speaker. As my friend Ivy Connor says:

> *There are only two keys to success: One is "get started."*
> *The other is "don't quit."*

1

Facing Fear

On July 12, 1987, while waiting to catch a plane in the Denver airport, I picked up a newspaper . On the front page was a story about the Reverend Billy Graham, the evangelist. The first two paragraphs read:

> *He has talked directly to an estimated 107 million people around the globe, and his friends figure he will speak to at least a quarter million more folks in Denver.*
> *But Billy Graham, the world's best-known preacher, **still gets nervous** before appearing in front of crowds.³ [Emphasis added.]*

Now I had an answer to the most frequently asked question in the briefing, presentation, and speech workshops I teach for executives, managers, and professionals.

> *QUESTION: How many people do you have to talk to before you stop getting nervous?*

> *ANSWER: I'm not sure, but since the answer is over 107 million, the odds of you or me getting there are not too good.*

I still have that paper (somewhat tattered now) and pull it out at the beginning of every class. Although the quote is very useful, it's not very surprising.

In one of my classes, I had a television reporter who could be seen at frequent intervals doing on-the-spot interviews for the evening news. (And doing them well.) She came to the class to learn how to handle fear. In another class I had a city council member from a large Denver suburb, and an assistant state attorney general who presented cases in court. They came for the same reason.

No one seems to be exempt; several years ago I asked a room full of professional speakers, "How many of you get nervous before giving a speech?" Every hand went up! Anyone who thinks that nervousness before a speech is uncommon should recall how many jokes there are about it.

At a retreat for managers of a large corporation and their spouses, the president's wife noticed the featured speaker pacing up and down. She tapped him on the shoulder.

"I didn't realize a famous speaker like you got nervous before a speech."

He snapped back: "I'm not nervous!"

"Then why are you in the ladies' room?"

If anyone tells you they aren't nervous before a speech, you have a right to be skeptical.

Anxiety Research

The phenomenon is so widespread, researchers have given it a name: *speech anxiety*, or sometimes, *communication apprehension* or *speech fright*. Interest in speech anxiety as a research topic is increasing rapidly, but the sensations are nothing new. The Roman orator Cicero (143-106 B.C.), acclaimed as the greatest speaker of his day, wrote, "I turn pale at the outset of a speech and quake in every limb and in all my soul."[4]

Not surprisingly, speech anxiety has physical, as well as mental, components. A group of medical researchers, seeking to find a link between coronary artery disease and mental stress, arranged a multi-stage test. Men with a history of coronary trouble were monitored while they exercised vigorously on a bicycle ergometer. They were then monitored during five difficult mental tasks. Four of the mental tasks produced no significant heart-function abnormalities, but the fifth task, giving a five-minute speech, was different. The researchers found:

> *Remarkably, the magnitude of abnormality induced by the most potent mental stress [of speaking] was not significantly different from that induced by vigorous exercise in the same patients.*[5]

That would not have seemed remarkable to Cicero.

Before you conclude that speaking should be banned as a health hazard, let's look at the implications of this finding. This research suggests a key to understanding speech anxiety and making it work for, not against, us. Our bodily systems do not discriminate between types of excitement. The holder of a winning ticket in a million-dollar lottery will experience the same physical symptoms (rapid pulse, high blood pressure, sweaty palms, among others) as the victim of armed robbery with a gun to his head.

If we could hook medical instruments on the lottery winner and the robbery victim, we would get similar readings on respiration changes, blood pressure, and the like. Therein lies the key. Any number of things can put us in an aroused emotional state. Since the bodily sensations for different emotions are approximately the same, the emotions we identify are largely determined by the context of the situation and our beliefs about that context. The emotions aroused by being robbed at gunpoint or cashing a winning ticket are obvious, but things are not as predictable for speakers.

The emotions generated by the challenge of presenting a speech can vary from ecstasy to despair. Which emotions we feel depend largely on our beliefs about the speaking situation. Good and bad speakers both feel the sensations which come with heightened emotions.[6] Bad speakers dread the sensations, interpreting them as signs of fear and obstacles to a successful speech. By contrast, good speakers feel the same sensations, but interpret them as signs of natural nervous energy – the same energy they need to sell themselves and their ideas to the audience. A good speaker is just as likely to be *psyched up* (nervous) before a speech as a good athlete is before a game. Those professional speakers I queried, who admitted they were nervous before a speech, expected to be nervous; they knew they would need to draw on that nervous energy to give a dynamic presentation. As one of his associates said of Billy Graham, "he doesn't get tense; he gets intense."[7]

Getting Intense

You, too, can get intense. Instead of wasting your time trying to fight off nervousness, you can convert that nervous energy into power and use it to drive home key points in your presentation.

When teaching this material in speech and briefing workshops, I sometimes hear this rebuttal:

Yeah, all this sounds good, but you can't make me believe

*everybody gets nervous. The last time I had to give a speech,
I was shaking. Then I looked around at the other speakers on
the platform and they were all cool and relaxed, like it was no
big deal.*

Most symptoms of anxiety are not obvious. You cannot see the butterflies in other speakers' stomachs, hear their hearts pounding, or feel the tightness in their chests. You won't know their palms are sweaty unless you shake hands. Even extreme symptoms like wobbly knees are likely to go unnoticed. If we were to ask a group of novice speakers to pick the most nervous person in the group, most would pick themselves because they would compare their inner sensations to the outward appearance of everyone else.[8] The truth is, most audiences can't tell you are nervous and wouldn't care anyway. Audiences will come to hear your ideas; whether your hands tremble is a matter of little importance.

Some speech coaches and consultants cling to the erroneous notion that people learn to speak well by being put under constant pressure. Their typical critique goes like this:

*You need to speak louder and stop fidgeting. I can tell
your hands are shaking because I heard the paper rattling.
Your introduction was too long, and whatever your main
point was, it was so obscure I couldn't tell. When you aren't
leaning on the podium, you pace back and forth, and your ear
must itch because you keep scratching it.*

People subjected to this bombardment tend to lose self-esteem, which creates even more fidgeting during the next speech.

I have found that if speakers concentrate on getting their ideas across and responding to the needs of the audience, most of the fidgeting takes care of itself.

Throughout the rest of this book you'll find tips for dealing with nervousness, but several suggestions are in order at this point.

First, when you sense nervousness before a speech, tell yourself, "this is the way it is supposed to feel. This is the energy I need to give a dynamic presentation." Then put it out of your mind and concentrate on your material and your audience.

Second, remember that giving a speech is like riding a bicycle.

The Mental/Physical Relationship

Speaking and bike riding are both complex activities in which mental and physical skills are interrelated. If you were teaching a child to ride a bike, you would have to teach certain basic mental principles:

Balance: "If the bike leans one way, you lean the other way."

Momentum: "Keep pedaling while you steer."

Traffic Awareness: "Watch for cars."

And so on.

But you wouldn't limit your instruction to mental principles; you would also have the child practice physical skills with some support. Perhaps, you would equip the bike with training wheels, or you would run alongside, holding the bike to steady it. Once the child successfully integrates the conceptual and physical aspects of bike riding, he or she is ready to ride alone.

From that point on, bike riding is basically a self-taught skill. The child gains skill and confidence through experience and gradually ventures into more difficult riding situations. Learning to give effective speeches and presentations is a similar process. You learn certain principles which apply in all situations:

Every good speech has a beginning, a middle, and an end.

Good speakers maintain eye contact with the audience.

You also develop concepts relating to a particular speech (main points, sub-points, examples). Then you practice until your mind and body learn to work together and you can give a well-coordinated speech.

Coping With Anxiety

Many would-be speakers err in thinking of speechmaking as if it were a purely mental activity. They carefully organize a speech as if it were a written proposal or journal article, perhaps even writing it out. They rehearse by repeating the speech silently to themselves a couple of times and then are overwhelmed by anxiety when they stand in front of an audience. The reason is simple. What is it we are afraid of when giving a speech? It's not the material, because we wrote that. What we are afraid of is the audience. We are afraid they will react with scorn or indifference or, worse yet, will laugh at us. If we rehearse merely by reading through the speech or by saying it into a mirror, the first time we face the object of our fear will be when we stand up to give the speech. No wonder it is overwhelming.

Think back to the bicycle analogy. If you had no experience with bikes but wanted to learn to ride so well you could ride to work down Main Street at rush hour, you could think of a number of bicycle-related activities to help you learn. You could read books on the subject and listen to bicycle experts talk. You could repeat the principles of bike riding to yourself. ("If the bike leans one way, I must lean the other way to straighten it.") You could buy an exercycle and pedal it in the basement. But if you went from the exercycle in the basement to Main Street at rush hour, you would either get run over or die of a heart attack. The most fearful thing about bike riding is the traffic, but thinking about biking principles and riding an exercycle do nothing to prepare someone for facing that fear.

Yet there are thousands of bike riders who safely ride in city traffic every day. The obvious difference is they have considerable experience in bike riding and have built their confidence by riding in increasingly difficult situations. They have not completely eliminated the anxiety caused by heavy traffic, but they use the anxiety to spur them to greater alertness. If your goal was to bike down Main Street at rush hour, a realistic practice schedule would have you go from the exercycle to a real bicycle in an empty parking lot (perhaps with training wheels). With no obstacles like streets and curbs, you could concentrate on keeping the bike up without having to pay much attention to steering. Once you felt secure in the parking lot, you would practice on an empty street, then on a street with a little traffic, then on a slightly busier street, and so on. When you eventually tackled Main Street at rush hour, your anxiety would be manageable since you had ridden the day before on a street almost as bad as Main.

Harnessing the Energy

Speakers can never eliminate anxiety completely, but they can learn to harness the nervous energy which fuels the anxiety and use it to give more dynamic presentations. A realistic rehearsal pattern for a speech resembles the bicycle-learning sequence. Start by mentally reviewing the speech outline until the ideas flow easily. Then, practice coordinating the physical and mental aspects so gestures and movements become second nature and visual aid changes flow smoothly. Finally, recruit a rehearsal audience so you can face the biggest fear of all as you rehearse in front of them. As with bike riding, dedicated physical and mental practice greatly increases confidence and skill. The relationships between physical and mental states are very complex and often surprising to those of us brought up on the traditional notion that the mind controls the body. It seems obvious that a speaker who speaks loudly is more confident than a speaker who whispers (assuming no sore throat). This fairly commonplace example illustrates how a mental state can affect physical performance. It is less well known, but easily proven, that the reverse is also true. A speaker can gain confidence by rehearsing loudly when he feels like whispering. That is, the physical act of talking loudly enhances the corresponding mental state (confidence).

The Last Word on Anxiety

If a speaker has a subject she believes in, has organized her material, and has rehearsed until she can deliver the speech forcefully and without hesitation, she will give an effective presentation, with or without anxiety.

Simple nervousness never stopped anyone who was motivated. If it did, no bride or groom would ever get through a wedding – or a wedding night.

Executive Summary

1. Everyone, including famous speakers, experiences heightened emotions before a speech.

2. Ineffective speakers identify their emotional state with nervousness and waste energy trying to fight off the feeling.

3. Effective speakers expect an emotional high and harness that energy to make a more dynamic presentation.

4. One key to gaining control over anxiety is gaining experience in facing the cause of the anxiety. For speakers that means rehearsing in front of a live audience, since the audience is the source of the anxiety.

2

Selling Yourself and Your Ideas

Imagine you are giving a speech on the dullest possible subject to the dullest possible audience. For me, the dullest situation I can imagine would be reading a profit and loss statement to the board of directors immediately after everyone had a big lunch. If profit and loss figures fascinate you, pick another situation. Then ask yourself what you are doing in this situation: are you just informing people or trying to sell something?

My high school speech teacher told the class all speeches were either informative, persuasive, or entertaining, and each type had its distinct requirements. I no longer believe there is such a thing as a purely informative speech. Even something as apparently informative as reading a profit and loss statement is actually persuasive. The speaker is trying to persuade the audience the figures are accurate. If you aren't selling anything else in a speech, *you are selling yourself and your ideas!*

Since every presentation you give will be an attempt at persuasion, your success rate will go up if you understand how people are persuaded.

In many ways, hearing a speech is like buying a used car. The customer on a used car lot is not only evaluating the cars. Since the salesman is his main source of information about the cars, he is evaluating the salesman, as well. In the same way, the speech audience is not only evaluating the information in the speech; they are evaluating the speaker, as well. If someone, a teacher for instance, critiques one of your speeches, you are likely to hear comments like these:

> *Don't jingle the coins in your pocket.*

> *I liked your use of the pointer.*

> *Don't pace back and forth. It's distracting.*

> *You need to talk louder.*

In a situation like that, you could easily get the impression that giving a good speech is just a matter of perfecting one set of mannerisms and avoiding other, potentially distracting, mannerisms. But the aim of every speech is to persuade, and audiences are not persuaded simply because you talk at the right volume and handle the pointer adroitly. The most polished speeches are not necessarily the most effective speeches. If you are to convince an audience, they must believe in your argument, believe in you, and be in the right frame of mind. Your own emotional state, the words you say, and the techniques you use are only tools to achieve those three objectives with the audience.

Aristotle on Persuasion

Aristotle understood all this 2200 years before anyone thought of selling a used car. He watched orators trying to sway the crowds in the streets of Athens, and he analyzed the tactics of those who were successful. He told his students a person could not persuade anyone unless three conditions were met:

> . . . *[1] the orator must not only try to make the argument of his speech conclusive and worthy of belief;*

> *[2] he must also make his own character look right, and*

> *[3] put his hearers, who are to decide, into the right frame of mind.*[9]

The starting point, of course, is to make your basic argument logical (''conclusive and worthy of belief''), a process which is explained more fully in the chapters on planning the speech. But Aristotle does not stop there.

Right Character: A successful speaker or used-car dealer must also "make his own character look right." No matter how sound the data looks, people will not believe it unless they trust the speaker's character. What does it take to generate that kind of trust? Listen to Aristotle again:

> *There are three things which inspire confidence in the orator's own character – the three, namely, that induce us to believe a thing apart from any proof of it:*
>
> *[1] Good Sense,*
>
> *[2] Good moral character, and*
>
> *[3] Good will*
>
> *False statements and bad advice are due to one or more of the following three causes:*
>
> *[1] Men either form a false opinion through **lack of good sense;** or*
>
> *[2] They form a true opinion, but because of their **moral badness** do not say what they really think; or finally,*
>
> *[3] They are both sensible and upright, but **not well disposed to their hearers**, and may fail in consequence to recommend what they know to be the best course.*
>
> *These are the only possible cases. It follows that anyone who is thought to have all three of these good qualities will inspire trust in his audience.[10] [Emphasis added.]*

Aristotle saw each of these failures in the would-be orators of his day. You and I can see the same faults on a used car lot:

1. Lack of good sense – the kid who is so dumb he tells you the car has fuel injection when you can look under the hood and see the carburetor. Would you believe him when he says it has a positraction rear end?

2. Moral badness – the guy who has you sign the contract and then fills in different options from what you agreed on.

3. Not well disposed (doesn't have your best interests at heart) – the

guy who is smart and honest but keeps trying to sell you the convertible with a high markup when he knows you need a station wagon to haul five kids and a dog.

Whether speaking to the public or to members of your own organization, you must avoid anything which would cast doubt on your own good sense, good moral character, or good will. You must never take quotations out of context, misconstrue opponent's arguments, or depend on unreliable sources.

In order for the audience to believe in your character, they must believe you are:

Smart enough to know the truth.

Honest enough to tell the truth.

Unselfish enough to support the true interests of the audience.

No doubt you are convinced of your own intelligence, honesty, and unselfishness, but you may be at a loss trying to figure out how to convince the audience of your sterling qualities. The easiest strategy would be to step behind the microphone and announce, "You should listen to me because I am the smartest person you will ever meet, and I know this subject inside and out." Since our culture considers that sort of straightforward approach to be self-serving, we need to approach the goal indirectly.

The first step is to determine what the audience believes about you. You may already know the audience well. (That's likely to be the case if you have spoken to them before or if they are a group within your own organization.) In case you don't know the audience, Chapter 3 and Appendix II can guide you in gathering information about them. For each of the personal qualities listed above (intelligence, honesty, unselfishness), you will find individual audience members hold one of three opinions:

They believe you have it. (That is, you are smart, etc.)

They believe you don't have it.

They haven't formed an opinion.

If you are lucky enough to have an audience which already believes you are smart and honest and support their interests, you won't need to spend time establishing your character. However, you will need to be careful not to sabotage their positive opinions of you. Self-sabotage, unfortunately, is easy to commit. To cast doubts on your own intelligence, you can confuse debits and credits, or say "Austria" when you obviously mean "Australia," or ask laid-off General Motors workers to buy stock in Toyota.

To raise questions about your honesty, take quotations out of context, or, better yet, invent quotations and attribute them to famous people. You can also present obsolete data as current, hide damaging information, or present fake credentials. (I once ran across an ad for an unusually cheap diploma mill and considered ordering a Ph.D. diploma for my dog, Senator Edmund Samusky. Unfortunately, at the time I couldn't spare $25.)

Should the audience be deceived into thinking you are unselfish enough to support their true interests, you can easily set them straight. Just leave your radio mike on while telling a confidant how gullible they are.

Gaining Credibility: An outside audience (that is, outside your normal contacts) may believe you are dumb, crooked, and selfish, but they are more likely to have vague, unformed opinions. Either way, you must establish your credibility before you can establish the logic of your position. Since you can't simply state how brilliant you are, you need to work in facts that imply it. Let's take several typical speech situations to see how it can be done.

Jayne Bartlett has been hired by a real estate developer to design a retirement complex to be built in a small town in the next state. Before the complex can be built, the city council must approve a zoning change, arrange for adequate utilities, and approve a waiver to the section of the building code which limits the number of occupants in a multi-family dwelling. The developer has arranged a special city council meeting, which is open to the public. During the meeting Jayne will be asked to explain and defend her design.

Jayne has a multi-faceted task. She must not only plan how to explain the design to people unfamiliar with architectural terms, she must also design visual aids to help the audience picture the finished complex. Equally important is the need to convince the audience she is a capable architect who genuinely wants to make their community a better place to live (in other words, she is smart and unselfish).

The developer will introduce Jayne, so Jayne briefs him in advance on the information she wants in her introduction. She wants him to say she has a master's degree in architectural engineering and also mention similar projects she has designed. She wants him to say these things because it would be awkward for her to work them in without seeming egotistical. She will reinforce the idea that she is smart by revealing some of her thinking during the design phase. ("We knew some of the residents would not have cars, so the main building will face south, reducing the distance residents will have to walk to go shopping.")

If she can, she will prove she has done her homework by telling the audience something they don't know about their community.

> *Several of the lots in this area have a surveying error because the older downtown area was platted by projecting lines from the survey points on the railroad right of way. By the time this newer area was developed from farm land, the surveyors worked from the grid that had been extended from the state capitol. The lines from the railroad don't match the lines from the capitol; there is a discrepancy of roughly ten feet.*

To help the audience believe in her honesty, Jayne can demonstrate her openness:

> *I mentioned the home in Junction City has a similar design. I checked with the administrator, and she would be happy for any of you to drive over and tour that facility.*

To help the audience understand she is unselfish enough to support their interests, Jayne will discuss those interests (to prove she knows what they are) and describe how she took them into account.

> *I know some of you in the immediate area are worried about overflow parking. You don't want a bunch of cars blocking the curb in front of your house.*
>
> *The off-street parking lots will be finished before the first occupant arrives. In calculating the size of the lots, we not only accounted for all the occupants' and staff members' cars, we added slots for cars for all the visitors we can accommodate and threw in a hundred extra slots so people won't have to park on the wrong side of the building.*

Remember the audience doesn't separate the character you show on the speaker's platform from the character you show in your office. If they can't believe you in one place, they won't believe you in the other.

Right Frame of Mind: Even if your argument is logical and your character above reproach, you may still fail to persuade unless you can place your audience in "the right frame of mind." Any audience will more easily accept the logic of your argument if they wish it were true. That's the reason so many speeches include touching anecdotes or pictures. One little girl with a game smile hobbling across the stage in leg braces will touch more hearts than a thousand statistics about birth defects.

Probably the most overlooked element in speeches by business and government leaders is emotion. Somehow, we have come to believe the only legitimate component of a speech is logic – all else is contraband. Nothing could be farther from the truth. The best speakers in any generation know how to blend logic with carefully selected emotional elements. Many do it so well the emotional appeals are virtually undetectable. The secret to using emotion well is understanding what it can do.

Remembering Aristotle said an audience could not be persuaded unless they believed the logic of the argument, trusted the speaker, and were in the right frame of mind, let's return briefly to the used-car analogy. Suppose you and your spouse are walking by a car lot when you see a car that looks perfect for your needs. A salesman steps up to tell you about the car. From the first few sentences you realize he is extremely knowledgeable about cars, is utterly trustworthy, and certainly has your best interest at heart. From what he says, you can see this car would be almost ideal. Despite all that, *if you are not in the mood to buy a car, you will not buy.*

Changing the Mood With Emotion: Perhaps you will find the audience receptive to you and your message. If so, you don't need to do anything to change their mood. But if they are not receptive, changing that mood becomes one of your top priorities, and emotion is the key to the change. If the salesman in the paragraph above wants to make a sale, he will get you to visualize moonlight drives in the new convertible or taking the family to Yellowstone in the new wagon.

Let's assume you have been asked to talk to a high school audience about automotive safety – practical things, like wearing seat belts and driving the speed limit. To a teenager, a car is just an extension of his personality. "You wanna be macho, you gotta drive macho." Definitely not an audience sympathetic to seat belts and speed limits. Before you get to the unpopular stuff, you need to change the mood:

> *I had a friend named Roger; we went through all twelve*
> *years of school together. His one goal in life was to be a pilot*

– an Air Force pilot, a Navy pilot, or an airline pilot. He had dreamed about that ever since he was a little boy.

When we were in high school, he got in a bad car wreck. He lived through it, but his right leg was smashed so bad it had to be amputated. Now his dream is gone forever.

I had another friend named Anita. Her family moved to town the year she started high school. Immediately, she was one of the most popular kids in school. She was not only beautiful outside; she was beautiful inside.

She was in a wreck, too. She lived, but her face went through the windshield. The doctors in the emergency room did the best they could, but she's no longer beautiful on the outside.

After a couple of stories like these, the audience's mood will be quite different – much quieter. Now when you talk about seat belts and speed limits, people will listen.

Even a subject which seems to be cold and analytical requires you to put the audience in the right frame of mind. Suppose you are the director of outside sales for POWERUP!, a company which supplies gasoline and diesel engines to companies drilling for oil and gas. Because of an industry slump, the president has directed all departments to reduce their staff by 20% and to reduce all non-personnel expenses by 30%. You have ten "service reps" who travel the oil and gas states to assess on-site needs, sell engines, and handle service problems. You have requested a meeting with the company president and senior staff to explain why the service rep positions should be exempt from the personnel cuts.

In this situation, you are likely to have many logical arguments. You can explain, for instance, how your people work 60-hour weeks. If you cut two positions without cutting the workload, people will burn out and quit. But logic alone won't work; the senior staff will have hardened themselves against that sort of argument. They will have convinced themselves that no matter how terrible conditions in different departments get, they must stick to their guns. Otherwise, the company will not survive.

Before you can convince them, you must change the mood. You can remind the staff that, in the minds of its customers, POWERUP! has always stood for quality service as well as a quality product; you can recall examples of customers switching from competitors because of your service reputation. You can remind them that the founder said he would rather have six customers and treat them right than have 600 and treat them badly. What is the point in surviving if you destroy the essence of the company? If we must fight to survive, let's at least go into battle with the banners high and fundamental values intact. Then with the audience in the right frame of mind (Quality above all!), you can talk about keeping the service reps.

To sell yourself and your ideas consistently, carefully evaluate each speaking situation to ensure your arguments are logical, your character trustworthy, and your cause desirable. And, remember the old saying, "A woman convinced against her will is of the same opinion still." It applies equally to men.

Executive Summary

1. Speeches which appear purely informative are actually persuasive because the speaker is selling himself and his ideas.

2. For an audience to be persuaded, they must not only believe the logic of the argument, they must also trust the speaker and be in the right frame of mind.

3. If the audience is to trust the speaker, they must believe she is smart enough to know the truth, honest enough to tell the truth, and unselfish enough to look out for the audience's best interest.

4. When the speaker finds an audience which is not in a receptive mood, he should tell stories with an emotional element to change the mood.

3

Assessing the Speaking Situation

The first step in planning a speech is to get a clear grasp of the occasion for the speech: Why are you speaking? Where? Who will be listening?

You can become committed to giving a speech or presentation in four different ways:

1. Someone directs you to speak. For instance, your boss may ask you to explain the environmental impact of a new project to a group of concerned citizens. You must either give the speech or risk disfavor by declining.

2. Someone invites you to speak. The local Chamber of Commerce might ask you to explain recent trends in your industry. In this type of situation, you have the option of declining.

3. You discover a need yourself and arrange a speech. If you felt employees needed information about impending policy changes, you could call a meeting and explain the changes to them.

4. You discover a need and volunteer your services to someone else. If you wanted to help high school students

understand your industry, you could volunteer to speak at a career night.

In each of these situations (except number 3) you have a contact person to work with. As soon as you can, after the first conversation with the contact, you need to find out details about the expected speech. To keep this information organized and not leave anything out, you can fill in a copy of the Speech Reservation Form in Appendix I. Much of the information requested on the form is routine and obvious (though still important). However, the questions highlighted in this chapter require more attention.

Speech Purpose

The most important thing to know when planning a presentation is why you are giving it. Knowing why you are to give a talk is more important that knowing what the talk is about. That is, the purpose is more important than the subject. Suppose you were asked to say a few words about your friend, Joe McGuire. The subject is obvious, but the purpose and the content of your speech would vary greatly depending on the occasion:

> At a *roast* in honor of his upcoming promotion, you would want to tell embarrassing stories.

> As a character witness at his tax evasion trial, you would stress his honesty and forthright character.

Most of your presentations will have a purpose which is harder to discern, but just as crucial. Missing the purpose could put you at the tax trial with nothing but a handful of off-the-wall anecdotes.

Discovering the purpose of a speech is basically a matter of deciding what you want the audience to believe or do. When you are assigned a presentation, you should ask what the purpose is, just as you would ask when and where it is scheduled.

A good statement of the purpose is specific and centered on the audience. "I want to tell my subordinates about the new computer network," is too vague. It names the subject, but gives no idea what you want to accomplish. "I want my subordinates to stop worrying that the new computers will be too difficult to operate," is better. It tells clearly what effect you wish the talk to have. Here are some other good purpose statements:

My objective is to persuade top management that my department should be spared from the proposed budget cuts.

I want to increase our staff's participation in the annual fund-raising campaign.

I want the prospective buyers to sign purchase contracts at the conclusion of the presentation.

I want the Rotary Club members to understand the vital role our company plays in the local community.

I want local farmers to volunteer to assist in our stream improvement program.

All of these are fairly open purpose statements, which could be shown to other members of your group. But you may also have other objectives which are covert:

I want my boss to realize how hard I have been working.

I want top management to question the judgment of my chief rival.

I want our customers to remember the poor service our competitors have given.

Whether these are valid objectives is for you to decide, but even if you have objectives no one else should see, you must still spell them out for yourself.

Planning a speech is a lot like planning a trip. If you don't pick a definite destination, there is no telling where you will end up.

The Audience as Individuals

Once you know the purpose, the most crucial thing to find out about a speech is who will be hearing it. The audience may be very familiar to you, or they may be unknown. In either case, what you know or can discover about the audience will have a major impact on your planning. Don't be afraid to ask others for information. The contact who assigns you or invites you to give a talk is likely to be a good source. I have not always gotten the information I needed, but I have never been rebuffed when asking for information about a prospective audience. Sometimes the contact doesn't have the information you need but can offer an educated guess. Since speaking is an inexact art, that educated guess can be quite valuable.

To keep the analysis as systematic as possible, try using the Audience Analysis Worksheet in Appendix II. The audience information you need will vary from speech to speech, so use the worksheet as a starting point. Since the reason for some questions is not always self-evident, the paragraphs below explain the connection of each bit of information to the speech planning process. As far as possible, you should determine these things concerning the audience:

Typical job positions and responsibilities: Where are they in the chain of command? Will what you are speaking about affect their jobs or is it only a matter of curiosity? How much power do they actually have? Can they do what you advocate?

What is their age range? Don't let your examples and phrases fall unnoticed into the generation gap. If you ask the audience to remember how they felt when Neil Armstrong stepped on the moon, you had better be sure they are all over 30. Conversely, if you are in your twenties talking to a group with some members in their forties, you must remember that OD used to mean a color and Ice-T was a drink.

Married or single? People with different life-styles have different interests and respond to different approaches. Stories about children will work well when speaking to the PTA, but not so well when speaking to the local singles ski club. Also, remember that some people are sensitive to questions about marital status; you may have to collect the information indirectly.

Percentage of men to women: While we want to avoid sexual stereotyping, we also want to connect with people on different wavelengths. One of the most common mistakes of male speakers is taking material that plays well with male audiences (i.e., sports and competition) and trying it with an audience of women *without making adjustments*. Although individual men and women differ dramatically from what is typical, groups of men and women seem to be fairly predictable in their interests. Women respond a little quicker to themes involving relationships; men respond a little quicker to themes involving competition. In a mixed group, men are likely to dominate the question and answer session, and women are more likely to pick up subtleties in language.

Strong beliefs/taboos: You may have heard that in Arab countries even left-handers eat with their right hands. To touch food with the (unclean) left hand is highly insulting. I heard professional speaker Tom Faranda say when he was speaking and banqueting in Saudi Arabia he sat on his left hand to avoid any momentary lapses. A North American traveling in the Mideast expects different customs and beliefs because even a casual glance down the street is a reminder of how different the place is. But traveling in North America does not provide those constant reminders of our differences, so a speaker may develop a false sense of security. We need to remember to look for the differences. There are companies in the Bible Belt where no one drinks socially. There are organizations in the mountain West whose managers avoid caffeine. There are even people who prefer living in densely forested areas, but hate the leading environmental groups (for eliminating timber industry jobs). Good speakers will search out these differences early in the process. Incidentally, the *Culturgrams* [sic], put out by a branch of Brigham Young University, provide a good, quick source for information on cultural expectations in other countries. (See the Resource List in the back of this book.)

Why is the audience coming to hear you? Because they want to? Or because they were forced? If they want to come, what do they hope to gain? If they were forced, how can you overcome their resistance?

What benefit do they expect from you? A heart-warming glow? Some funny jokes? A solution to a maddening problem? You need not be tied to the audience's expectations, but you must start with those expectations before you can lead them anywhere else.

Other expectations? Some expectations are negative. If you are from the South and the audience isn't, they may expect you to be a warmed-over Scarlett O'Hara or Colonel Sanders. If you represent a church, the audience may expect a "goody-two-shoes." If you are in the military, they may expect you to growl like General Patton. In any situation where the audience's expectations are off the mark, you need to concentrate on slaying the stereotype before you can build your own credibility.

Are they for or against your position? Are you aiming to change their minds or merely to reinforce what they already believe?

Other things they may be worrying about: You may have a great speech for selling investment planning to teachers, but if the superintendent

plans to stand up before your talk and announce a salary freeze and involun-
tary terminations, you may want to reschedule. Worries on any subject, even
a trivial subject, will make your job harder because people will be distracted.
To keep a worried audience with you, you need to hit harder on the points
that touch them, keep up the pace and the energy level, and keep the
presentation short.

**Generally, how educated are they and how much do they know
about your particular topic?** Most of the time you will know more than
your audience. If you didn't, someone else would give the speech. Many a
speaker has forgotten that fact and drowned the audience in a sea of
specialized terms and acronyms. Even a highly educated audience can be
uninformed on your particular topic. If in doubt, simplify!

What is their interest in the topic? The answer can range from
"none at all" to "the most critical issue we face." The lower the audience's
interest level, the more effort you must devote to demonstrating that the
topic is interesting or important.

Jargon and terms they use frequently: The audience will accept
your credibility much quicker if you can talk like a knowledgeable insider.

Any language difficulties? (English as a second language, etc.) An
international trainer told me when he did seminars in the English language in
Singapore and Bangkok, he had to stop after every sentence to allow the
better English speakers to translate for their friends. If you expect any
language difficulties, you should be prepared to shorten your presentation
and you should reinforce what you say by visual means. Have a slide for
every main point and consider having supplemental handouts.

What values are important to them? A political speech on the need
to defend social security can be expected to play well at a retirement home,
but not on a college campus. If you need to challenge your audience's
values, you must build your case very carefully.

What constraints does the audience have? Are the actions you
propose within their power?

What mood will you find them in? Is it conducive to your speech or
will you have to change the mood?

What physical state will they be in? Put an audience in a warm room right after lunch and even the best speakers will have to battle to keep them awake. I once showed a movie to one of my Bradley University classes right after lunch and asked everyone to stand during it. My strategy wasn't good enough – one student fell asleep while standing. If you anticipate the audience will be too hot, too tired, too dusty, or too drunk, try to change the arrangements. Offer to speak at another time, if necessary. If you are forced to deal with an audience in bad shape, use a lot of audience participation to keep them with you.

What has worked with this group in the past? How can a speaker touch them to establish rapport? What has moved them to make a favorable decision? If you can find out what has worked before and it's within your repertoire, by all means, play to that strength.

What are they likely to wear? While this may seem like an odd question at first, it is actually one of the more important ones on this list. You don't need to dress exactly like the audience members, but you don't want to look totally different. You should have some common ground. Imagine this scenario: your boss asks you to pitch one of your organizations's key projects to a group of bank executives at their summer retreat. Since you know the bankers to be reserved and conservative in dress, you appear at the retreat in your three-piece suit (or, if you prefer, a tailored jacket, blouse, and skirt). However, the annual retreat is one of the few chances the bankers have to dress casually. They are all in shorts and tank tops. Your best response is fairly obvious. Take off your jacket and tie or scarf, roll up your sleeves, and go to work. You won't look like them, but at least they can tell you know it is a casual occasion. They may even think you came straight from the office and didn't have time to change.

Let's assume you did so well on that occasion your boss sends you to another retreat with another group of bankers. Remembering your last mistake, you show up in shorts, shower clogs, and the Hawaiian shirt your brother-in-law brought back. After driving 100 miles you step in the lodge and discover this group of bankers never step out of character. They are all in tailored suits with stiffly starched shirts. Now, how do you adjust?

The best way to prevent this sort of fiasco is to get the best information you can and then dress one step better than you expect the audience to dress. Adjusting downward is easy.

The Audience as a Group

Some audiences are a random assembly; people in the audience have never seen each other before. Other audiences see themselves as a group with a distinct history and group personality. If you are going to address an established group, you need to know how the group typically functions and how the members see the group. More precisely, you should find out:

Organizational history: Find out, not just what has happened in the past, but what current members say about the past. Every worker at J. C. Penney stores learns that J. C. Penney believed his success was due to following the Golden Rule and treating every employee as a partner. Students at Fort Lewis College learn that it is different from other state colleges in Colorado, for it began as a boarding school for Indians on nearby reservations. Although the school's mission has changed, Native Americans can still attend tuition-free.

Bits of information like these provide valuable insights into group values. Penney's executives are likely to be responsive to an appeal to basic fairness, and the Fort Lewis administration will probably look positively on initiatives for new multi-cultural programs.

Current challenges: Your informant with the host organization will be more comfortable talking about challenges than problems. Either way, the people at the top (and, perhaps, those at the bottom) will be looking for ways to fix the problems and face the challenges. If you can help with the fixing or the facing, you will have their undivided attention.

Organizational structure: You want to know about the informal structure, as well as the formal organizational chart. You want to know who people listen to in casual conversation. Who makes decisions and who only recommends decisions? Is the structure rigidly hierarchical or fluid and democratic? Answers to these questions help you decide where to pitch your arguments. Audience members are rarely equal; make certain you address the concerns of the most important members.

Recent Successes: Normally, you want the audience in a positive mood – so congratulate them on landing the big contract, or getting recognized by the presidential commission. While you are at it, it doesn't hurt to point out similarities between the actions you propose and those that led to the recent victory.

Size: Are the ten people in your audience the entire organization or just a fragment of the board of directors? You need to talk about what is possible. Huge organizations are typically powerful but ponderous; smaller organizations tend to be light and quick. Survival dictates different strategies and tactics. Make sure what you say fits the environment the group is in.

Organizational mission or goals: If you want to have any input into their decisions, you must understand where they think they are going. Whether you are selling plain-paper copiers, accounting software, or just ideas, your approach to an association of beer distributors will differ from your approach to an association of Christian booksellers.

The mission statement of the U. S. Forest Service is lengthy and rarely quoted, but every employee has memorized the Forest Service motto: *Caring for the land and serving people.* If you are trying to sell a proposal to any group within the Forest Service, you would to well do show how your proposal supports those two goals.

Organizational self-image: Self-image is closely related to mission, but it includes another element. Self-image includes not only where they want to go (mission), but what they are willing to do to get there (ethics). Suppose the audience is a family. Most families have a goal of earning more money than they presently have. Some families are willing to commit armed robbery to get rich. Other families won't stoop to violence but consistently cheat on their taxes. Still other families are scrupulously honest, but will work very hard. Others will work, but not very hard. And, of course, there are others whose efforts to get rich are confined to playing the lottery.

Most groups are very reluctant to do anything contrary to their self-image. Once you understand what the audience's self-image is, you need to study your ideas, to see where they are compatible with that self-image. Then stress the points you have in common.

Recent disasters: On March 15, 1991, I was in Perth, Australia, trying to hold a public seminar, which was rather difficult because half of those who pre-registered were an hour late. It turned out that a small group of farmers, angry about U.S. subsidies of wheat exports, had shut down rush hour traffic by parking and locking rented trucks in the middle of freeway choke points.

As a loyal U.S. citizen, I defended our government's export policy the best way I knew how – I didn't mention it!

Whenever a group you represent is at odds with the audience, you will find yourself in one of two positions. Either you are charged with negotiating the sore point, or you aren't. *If the point of contention isn't on your agenda, leave it alone!* In situations like this one, nothing you say can help you, and anything you say opens a potential minefield.

The trouble is many of these minefields are camouflaged. Before I left for Australia I read everything I could find about current events, especially politics. There was no mention of angry wheat farmers. I felt less like a dunce nine months later when President Bush was blind sided by the same issue on his Australian trip in January 1992. After all, he had people who were paid to steer him past this kind of hazard.

If explosive public issues like the wheat subsidy can go undetected, it is even easier for private disasters to hide in the underbrush. Consider these possibilities: As the director of a social service coalition, you are speaking to the Chamber of Commerce, soliciting contributions to establish a safe house for battered women. The president of the Chamber turns red and stomps out. Then someone hands you a note saying the president has just been slapped with a restraining order requested by his ex-wife.

Or perhaps you have put together a portfolio of attractive international investment opportunities at the request of a group of financiers. When you mention that the prime attraction of the portfolio is a chance to finance the start of a major factory on the Pacific Rim, the atmosphere changes from warm to icy. Later you learn the group lost millions when the previous government in the same Pacific Rim country nationalized one of their factories.

Collecting enough information to prevent this kind of self-injury is difficult, because people are reluctant to talk about bad memories. If the collection effort seems more difficult than it is worth, imagine yourself walking through the minefield.

Whether the organization is growing or shrinking: Determining this point will tell a lot about the atmosphere you will encounter. If the organization is expanding, people are likely to have good morale despite heavy workloads. If the organization is shrinking, employees are likely to be focussed on diminishing opportunities and possible termination.

Who does the organization compete with? Executives and managers are likely to find their view of reality colored by the competition. If you are speaking to a small organization whose markets are being invaded by a massive competitor, your audience is likely to display a siege mentality. On the other hand, if you speak to a group which has succeeded by staying one step ahead of the competition, they will want you to cut out the fluff and get to the decision point.

Who are the key people? You need to know the key people in the organization and the key people in the audience (in case they are not the same). Whose advice is listened to? Who makes the decisions and how do they arrive at a conclusion? What are their main concerns and how can you address those concerns?

Where You Can Find Out

Your contact with the organization: The person who contacted you about speaking normally has a vested interest in seeing you succeed. He or she can answer many of the questions listed above and can also put you in touch with other resources.

Current employees or volunteer workers: If you need to understand a job, ask the people who do it. Some time ago, I was asked to provide training for Postal Service supervisors in a particular region. They needed specific help in dealing with troublesome employees. Since I have never been a Postal Service employee and have only an outsider's knowledge of the various work routines, I could only guess at the sorts of things troublesome employees might do. To fill the gaps in my knowledge, I asked a senior manager to give me names and phone numbers for several supervisors who were exceptionally good at dealing with trouble. My calls to those supervisors were invaluable. After I explained why I needed the information, they were frank and specific. I came away with a much clearer understanding of the problems facing supervisors in that field.

Former employees or volunteers: Current employees may have a vested interest in hiding or coloring certain types of information. Former employees will have less interest in protecting the organization. However, if you hook up with someone who has an ax to grind, you should not accept every statement at face value; try to confirm critical points from another source.

Competitors: This source can be valuable, but tricky to work with. A competitor who keeps close tabs on the rest of the industry can often validate information you get from other sources. Some competitors also take pleasure in recounting someone else's recent disasters. Contacting a competitor can be tricky if you have a client relationship with the group you are speaking to. You don't want to arouse suspicions about your loyalty. In that situation, you must not break a confidence, or reveal proprietary information – or even look like you might. Professional association meetings can provide a neutral ground on which you can ask a competitor a few casual questions without arousing suspicion.

Previous speakers: Someone who has spoken to the same group, or worked with them in another capacity is likely to have the kind of information you need. If you aren't aware of anyone who has spoken to the group before, ask your contact person what speakers they have had before.

Brochures and newsletters: Any publication with an in-house circulation can provide hints about current issues and trends, and you may pick up background information on key people. Ask your contact or the organization's public affairs office to send back issues of these publications and to put you on the mailing list.

Standard reference works: Any organization which has been in existence for more than a couple of years will have background information in sources open to the public. The most likely sources are libraries, professional or industry associations, and chambers of commerce. The quickest way to get open-to-the-public information is to call the reference librarian at the biggest library in your area, explain what you want to find, and ask how to find it. Some reference librarians will even look up the information for you, if they are not too busy.

Newspaper files and editors: The business editor of a local paper may have in memory what you need to know about a local organization. If not, someone can check the newspaper files to find the stories that paper has done on a particular organization.

Questionnaire: Depending on the circumstances, you can send a questionnaire to all the audience members, to a sample of audience members, or just to your contact. Some professional speakers rely heavily on questionnaires. To increase the chances of getting it back, a questionnaire should be simple to fill out, i.e. have boxes to check instead of requiring lengthy comments.

Ask the Audience: For most speeches and presentations, if you arrive early you will have a chance to chat with audience members before the meeting convenes. Seize this opportunity if you possibly can; now you can talk to the people who will actually be hearing you. Although you can gather excellent information while conversing with the audience, you should not rely on this method as your primary source, unless you plan on rewriting your speech ten minutes before you give it. You can make minor changes at the last minute, but if your advance information is sound, you should not encounter any major surprises.

Scouting the Location

Planning a speech is like planning a guerrilla war: it pays to know the terrain. If you are scheduled to give a presentation in a place you don't know well, try to visit the location ahead of time. In addition to getting a feel for the atmosphere of the place, you need answers to some specific questions:

How good are the acoustics? In other words, can you speak without a microphone? Sound bounces off hard surfaces and is absorbed by soft surfaces. Always remember, audience members are soft surfaces. A room which echoes when empty will most likely not echo when full of people. By the same token, to be heard in the back of the room will require more volume as the room fills up with people.

Is the room suitable for what you intend to do? Several years ago I was conducting a presentation workshop in a hotel, which I had never used before, on the west side of metro Denver. Speeches by the participants were videotaped, so they could see themselves as the audience saw them. When the tapes were played back, the speakers' voices were drowned by audio static. Through trial and error we discovered the tapes would play back sans static if the playback was in an interior room without windows. Apparently, something in the area was generating radio waves, which were picked up by the unshielded connecting cable between the VCR and TV. The next time I had a workshop booked into a west side hotel, I hauled my equipment in the week before to test it. Although this problem is rather bizarre, it illustrates what can happen when an unexpected problem surfaces.

Other things to check for: Is the ceiling high enough to accommodate a projection screen? If not, you will need to change rooms or plan the speech without slides or overhead transparencies. Will you be confined to the stage or can you move down the aisles while speaking? Is your 35mm slide carousel compatible with their 35mm projector?

What equipment will be available? Microphone? Projector? Screen? Extension cord? Before I got in this business I assumed any large, respectable hotel would have plenty of extension cords, but some of them don't. This would be a good time to run a preliminary test of the equipment and check for spare bulbs.

Where will equipment be placed? See Appendix V for different room arrangements. Putting the screen in a corner usually provides better sightlines for the audience. If you already have slides, check to see if they can be read. Most important, try to find the person who will be in charge of setting up the room and explain where you want everything.

If you are giving a speech out of town, all of these steps will be more difficult. You should still ask all the necessary questions and consider having a proxy check details at the location.

Executive Summary

1. The most important thing to know when planning a presentation is why you are giving it. What is the purpose of the presentation?

2. At the beginning of your speech planning, write down the objectives you want the speech to accomplish. Be specific.

3. Using your contact for the speech, along with other sources, find out as much as you can about the types of individuals who will be in the audience.

4. Find out as much as you can about the organization you will be addressing.

5. Scout the speaking location ahead of time to ensure it is suitable for what you intend to do.

6. Check the acoustics to see if you will need a microphone.

7. Determine what other equipment will be available.

8. Arrange for placement of equipment. Putting the screen in a corner usually provides better sightlines for the audience.

4

Roughing Out the Speech

Gathering material for a speech is a lot like shopping at the supermarket: it helps to have a list of what you want. If you know what you are looking for, you will find it a lot quicker. So before you do any serious research, you need to develop a rough outline of what you want to say. Later, when you dig up background material and evidence to support your points, you may find a need to modify what you plan to say. When you start rehearsing the speech, you may want to drop some points because of time constraints. Even if the odds are high you will change it later, you still need a rough outline at the beginning to aid your search for material. To keep the speech planning process as orderly as possible, I have developed the *ComSkills* Speech Planner, which you will find in Appendix III.

Go to the *ComSkills* Speech Planner now and make an enlarged copy of it to keep at hand as you read the rest of this chapter and the other chapters on planning. Individual parts of the Planner are inserted at different points in these chapters and are then explained, but it is easier to understand the whole process if you see the Planner altogether.

1. PURPOSE: What do you want the audience to do as a result of your speech? Be specific.

Everything you do in preparing a speech, briefing, or presentation should be goal-driven. That is, you decide at the beginning what you want to accomplish and then choose the strategies and evidence to achieve that goal. As pointed out in the preceding chapter, the purpose of a speech may be dictated or you may have some choice. Either way, you need to list the purpose at the top of the first page of the Planner and keep it in mind as you work through the other steps.

NOTE: Before proceeding, take a separate sheet of paper and brainstorm the speech, listing all the ideas you can think of that relate to this purpose.

You need to think of all the things you *could* say before deciding what you *will* say. Remember, Aristotle said the audience could be convinced only if they accepted the logical argument, trusted the speaker, and were in the right frame of mind. Because your ultimate goal is to persuade the audience, you are not just searching for cold facts to build a logical argument. You are also looking for ways to build trust and for things that will touch the audience to put them in a receptive frame of mind.

Mind-Mapping

The whole process of researching and organizing a speech should result in one product: the short outline you will speak from. But you should not attempt to start with the outline. A few gifted people have the ability to organize a speech completely in their heads and then merely scribble down a few notes. But most people who attempt to start with the outline they will finally use end up with either a very disorganized outline or nothing (due to writer's block).

A better approach is to generate ideas and collect support before attempting to organize the outline. The traditional method for generating ideas is to sit down with a pencil and paper and rapidly jot down every possible idea, paying no attention to the order. An improvement on that is to sit down with several other people who are familiar with the subject and bounce ideas around. Getting more than one mind to work on the task will normally result in more and better ideas. An even better approach is mind-mapping.

Mind-mapping is a recent improvement on the traditional process of generating ideas. It was invented by Tony Buzan, founder and director of the Learning Methods Group in England.[11]

The strength of mind-mapping comes from its ability to transcend the normal linear nature of language. The outline you ultimately produce and the speech you ultimately give have a basically linear structure. You present one idea followed by another, which is followed by another, and another, and another – as if they were beads on a string.

The problem is that many of the subjects you might talk about are non-linear. Suppose you were scheduled to talk on ''Ways to Improve Employee Performance.'' You might generate a linear list of sub-topics like this:

Training

Better supervision

Recruiting more skilled people

Better operating instructions

Simplify tasks

Writing the list this way implies linear relationships: it implies *supervision* logically follows *training* and precedes *recruiting*. But *supervision* could just as easily follow *simplify tasks* because a simpler task will require less supervision of the worker. While each of these sub-topics has some relationship to the others, they all are closely related to improving performance, but the simple list does not show these relationships clearly.

Mind-mapping allows you to display relationships visually as ideas occur to you. Because the creative part of your mind is spatially oriented, scanning the visual framework will stimulate you to generate more ideas.

The process of creating a mind-map is rather simple. Sit down with a very large sheet of paper. A piece of flip-chart paper or the back of a sheet from a giant-sized desk calendar/blotter would be ideal. Print the speech topic in the middle and draw a box around it.

Improve
Performance

Then search your mind for a related topic. As topics occur to you, print each one and draw lines to show where it fits in the overall design. Only the main idea gets a box. The others are circled. When I was teaching at the Air Force Institute of Technology, a student of mine, Captain Bill Hippenmeyer, suggested labeling the connecting lines with verbs to suggest what the exact relationships are. The map below (Figure 4-1) shows one way of connecting the ideas from the list on the previous page. Many variations are possible, of course.

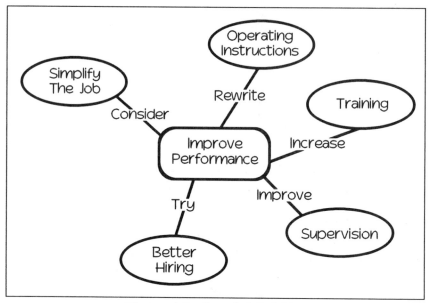

Figure 4-1 - Sample Mind-Map

As each new idea occurs to you, study the map to find the most logical place for it. Doing the map in pencil will let you change it easily. Consider what might happen on the right side of our sample (Figure 4-2). There are several possible ways to improve supervision: train the present supervisors, hire additional supervisors, or put more pressure on the supervisors to enforce production standards. Several interconnections occur: hiring supervisors presents similar problems to hiring better workers; and training supervisors is logically connected to training workers.

You should be able to see by now why large sheets of paper are required. To complete the mind-map you simply keep adding ideas and drawing connections until you have the whole subject covered. Then, put the points in a logical, linear order while editing out the ones you don't need.

Most people who use mind-maps find they stimulate creativity – it takes less time to think of all the ideas you need for a speech. Because it allows you to see the whole pattern of connected ideas at a glance, a mind-map also aids in outlining. It is easy to scan the map for the next logical topic. (As an alternative, an outline processor program for your computer will let you accomplish some of the same things with a totally different methodology.)

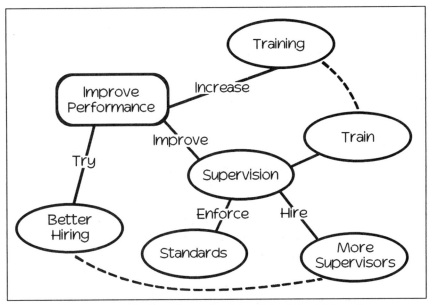

Figure 4-2 - *Expanding the right side of the Mind-Map diagram.*

What you are jotting down on the mind map are simply key words that represent ideas. Some of the ideas will be close at hand in your own memory (a joke, for instance). At other times, you will think of an idea, but will not know or be able to remember all the relevant data (like last year's inventory figures). In that case, jot down the idea and look up the data later. If you have trouble thinking of anything related to your speech topic, scan the following list for ideas.

Analogies: Think of a similar situation to illustrate the one you are talking about.

A computer database is organized like a metal filing cabinet. In a filing cabinet all information relating to Furni-

*ture For Less, Inc. would be put in a file folder labeled with
the company name. In a database, all information relating to
Furniture For Less would typically go in a record labeled
with the company name.*

Analogies which work well are always based on something very
familiar to the audience. In the example above, the filing cabinet should be
familiar to virtually all adults. The example below violates this principle
and, therefore, won't work with an average audience.

*On a map of linguistic dialects, an "iso-graph" serves
the same function as an isotherm on a weather map.*

Anecdotes: Use a story to illustrate a point. It could be humorous or
serious. Try to find connections with your audience. An audience will be
much more interested in this opening, "As I was driving north of town here
on Route 675 . . ." than in this one, "A man was driving down the highway
once when . . ."

An anecdote derived from your own experience will normally be more
effective than one borrowed from a speech you heard. Telling about your
daughter's struggle with cerebral palsy may sound tame compared to another
speaker's story about struggling up Mount Everest. But you can make your
daughter's story come alive for an audience; you will find it much harder to
make Mount Everest come alive because you weren't there. If you do use
borrowed anecdotes, credit the source to protect your own credibility.

Authority: Bolster your case by citing a recognized expert.

*Ninety percent of the politicians give the other ten percent
a bad reputation.*

Henry Kissinger[12]

Definitions: Obviously essential for your key terms, but useful
elsewhere, as well. People are usually fascinated by the meanings and
origins of words. In a speech on the right to privacy, you might explain the
etymology of the word *eavesdrop.*

*In earlier centuries "eavesdrop" was pronounced
"eavesdrip." The eavesdrip (quite logically) was the water
which dripped off the eaves of a house before the average
house had gutters. Eavesdrip also meant the ground that*

water fell on. Anyone who stood closer to your house than the eavesdrip was presumed to be invading your privacy.

Examples: Consider all the possibilities – from stories ("Here is one case where the new safety equipment prevented a lost-time accident.") to physical objects ("This cracked fitting is an example of what can happen when a torque wrench is out of specs."). As with other types of evidence, the closer the example is to the audience, the better.

This uzi machine gun was confiscated less than ten blocks from here. The police took it from a teenager who had it concealed under his jacket.

Facts: Be ready to back them up by giving your sources. You should also work at stating the facts in a way that will be easily remembered.

Communication technology is reshaping the globe. Using a fax machine, I can get a letter from North America to Australia in less time than it takes to run the same letter across the street to a business without a fax.

Figures: Figures are facts in statistical form. Don't drown the audience with numbers; too many speakers try to prove a point by showing screen after screen of small-print numbers. To succeed with statistics, you need to pare them down and transform them from disembodied abstractions into something real that the audience can relate to.

Suppose you need to send a note to your affiliate in Atlanta. You know how much it costs to mail a letter and how long it takes the letter to arrive. I can fax that letter to Atlanta in 25 seconds at a cost of 23 cents. That's the rate for business hours; in the evening it costs 13 cents.

Jokes: These can be very effective, but make sure the humor is pertinent to the point you are making. To illustrate the need for careful phrasing you could tell this story.

A soldier injured in the Gulf War was recuperating in an Army hospital. Since both his arms were in casts, a kindhearted nurse offered to help him write a letter to his wife.
"The nurses here," he dictated, "are rather plain looking."

"That's really unfair!" declared the nurse.
"Of course it is, but it will make my wife very happy."

Quotations. Quotes can be prose or poetry. You can quote anyone from the guy who roofs your house, to Abraham Lincoln. No matter who said it, the quote must be pertinent and memorable. If the quote is clever, or at least short and snappy, so much the better.

The secret of business is to know something nobody else knows.

Aristotle Onassis[13]

War is too important to be left to the generals.

Georges Clemenceau[14]

Most of the companies that have a union deserve one.

Ross Harlan

The more you sweat in peace, the less you bleed in war.

Chinese proverb

Serious Research: Gathering the Evidence

The evidence you need to convince the audience may be in your mind or stacked in your office, or it may be hidden, waiting for someone to search it out. If the evidence requires a search and you don't have time to do the searching, consider hiring a researcher. To find a good one, ask your contacts in academic circles and industry groups for recommendations. Professional associations for speakers and writers are also good hunting grounds. To save some money, hire a graduate student from your local university. Try to find one with a lot of initiative who is studying in your field or in library science. Most department heads would be in a position to give you some names.

Whether you are doing your own research or pointing a hired researcher in the right direction, you should think about alternate sources and shortcuts. The summer between my sophomore and junior years in college, I owned 50% of Flamingo Lawn Service. My partner, Bill Buschhorn, and I invented a method for finding prime markets for lawn mowing. We would cruise around until we found a neighborhood with expensive homes and no bicycles. No bicycles meant no teenagers; the man of the house had no choice but to mow the lawn himself or hire someone. (This occurred before women were liberated into lawn mowing.)

Don't get sucked into thinking valuable research only occurs in the laboratory or the library. Actually, some of the most effective research, especially speech research, is informal. If you want to know the best-selling perfume in your area, you can wait a month for the industry report – or you can ask the clerks at perfume counters. If you want to know last year's vacancy rate for leased office space in your area, you can spend an hour at the library thumbing through statistical summaries, or you can call the Chamber of Commerce and ask. Anytime you want to know anything, ask yourself if there isn't someone who would have a vested interest in collecting that information. Then call.

If you do need library research and haven't been in a library for a few years, you may not realize how much things have changed. Before you spend time in a library building, ask about electronic shortcuts. With my computer and a modem, I can get free access to a system which will locate any book or article in any library in central Colorado. For a small fee, I can have a librarian search most of the country. Unless you enjoy burrowing through library stacks, you can save yourself time and frustration by telling a librarian what you are searching for and then taking advantage of any suggested shortcuts.

After you have your hands on the information you researched, you should return to your mind-map to plug in and connect the new material.

Writing a speech is like gathering hay. The stuff isn't much use until you bale it. Once you have gathered enough material, you are ready to organize the speech, which is covered in the next chapter.

Executive Summary

1. The first step in roughing out a speech is deciding exactly what you want the audience to do as a result of the speech.

2. The second step is brainstorming or mind-mapping to come up with a long list of possibly useful ideas.

3. You may need to supplement the information from your memory with information gained from serious research. If your time is limited, consider hiring a researcher.

5

Organizing to Persuade

The Audience

Speeches with power are audience-centered. The speaker designs the speech to fit what is on the minds and hearts of the audience. An observer can't be sure if the speaker motivated and sold the audience, or just opened the door and let them motivate and sell themselves. To build that kind of presentation, you need to focus on the audience and their needs early in the process. Let's return to the *ComSkills* Speech Planner.

2. KEY PLAYERS: Describe the principal decision-makers in the audience.

Name	Position	Decision-making Role

Look at your audience analysis. Working from your collected information, list the most important people on the Planner. Remember that a person's decision-making role for your presentation may not correspond to the position. If you are trying to sell an organization a $1.5 million computer system, the head of Data Processing is likely to play a more prominent role than normal. When you have identified the key players and understand what makes them tick, you are ready for the most important of all audience questions: *What is in it for them?*

3. MOTIVATION: Why should audience members care about your topic? What will they gain by doing what you want?

Before people will change their minds or do anything else voluntarily, they must believe they will be better off after the change. What makes them feel better may be something tangible, like a new copier that doesn't eat originals; or it may be intangible, perhaps self-satisfaction from helping provide homes for families in Panama. If a decision-maker can't visualize her world being somehow brighter (or at least less dreary) from doing what you advocate, inertia will stop her cold.

On the Planner, write down what the audience will gain so you will be sure to make it clear to them.

4. MAJOR POINT: State *in one sentence* the most important idea you want the audience to remember.

You already know what you want the audience to do (Purpose) and you know why they will want to do it (Motivation). Now decide what the audience must believe in order to act. Consider this example:

> PURPOSE: I want the audience to replace their old data storage system with the new one I am selling.

> MOTIVATION: They will have less down-time, therefore less frustration.

> MAIN POINT: The Burns 1100 is by far the most reliable and trouble-free data storage system in its class.

Notice how the audience's motivation led to the main point in this example.

Here's another way of looking at it. If they forgot everything you said except one sentence, what would you want that sentence to be? What is the one thing above all else that you want the audience to believe. Don't settle for two or three things: one point must be pre-eminent; the others are support. If you don't design the speech with a single aiming point, it will lack focus. Study your mind map until you have decided on the main point; then write it down. Remember that all great speeches have very simple themes. Consider these:

> *Old soldiers never die. They just fade away.*
> Douglas MacArthur

We have nothing to fear, but fear itself.
> Franklin Delano Roosevelt

I have a dream!
> Martin Luther King, Jr.

5. OBJECTIONS: List likely objections and how you will answer them.

Objection	My Approach

Ronald Reagan's management style, according to observers, was focused on big issues. He let others take care of the details to such an extent he rarely knew what the details were. But at press conferences he was transformed. No matter what the issue raised by a journalist, he could respond with an overview of the big picture followed by a clear discussion of all the pertinent details. How could he do it? What made him utterly different when he stepped in front of a TV camera?

He simply did what other presidents have done before press conferences. He held rehearsals at which staff members asked every conceivable question and suggested possible answers. Alternate answers would be debated and the best ones rehearsed and refined as the president committed them to memory. Every modern president has prepared in the same way, but having myriad details on the tip of the tongue at a press conference was no change of pace for someone like Jimmy Carter, whose management style was always focused on details.

The rehearsal process is obviously labor intensive, therefore expensive. Whether you should attempt a full-blown rehearsal and analysis of every answer is really a question of return on investment. Ask yourself what is at stake in an upcoming speech. Quantify what you hope to gain. Then calculate the labor cost of an intensive rehearsal-analysis session. Compare the two figures to see if you are making a reasonable investment. Suppose the payoff does not justify a heavy investment of staff time – you should still think through the process carefully.

Good audience analysis will help you understand what the audience already believes on the subject. If objections to any of your points are likely, you should know what the objections are and who will raise them. With that foreknowledge, you can choose an appropriate strategy.

With an objection which is petty, obviously biased, or illogical, you may not wish to respond. Every gripe does not deserve an answer. In general, an objection which does not threaten any of your key points and does not capture the approval of the audience may safely be ignored.

If you anticipate an objection which does threaten your case, you must refute it, either in the speech or in the question period. Explaining the objection and refuting it in the body of the speech keeps everything orderly and ensures the objection will be worded the way you want it. On the other hand, your answer will have more impact if you hold your material in reserve and spring it on a questioner.

What if you know of other objections which are not likely to come up? Should you ignore them or bring them up and refute them? To answer that question, estimate the likelihood that decision-makers in the audience will encounter these objections from another source later. Suppose you are a Forest Service district ranger scheduled to meet with a local environmental group to explain and defend a proposal to open part of your national forest district to snowmobiling. You expected the group to be concerned about possible damage to a fragile environment, so you structured the proposal to limit such damage. You intend to restrict snowmobiling to established roads and trails when they are icy or snow-packed. Snowmobilers may not take their machines into open meadows, and the activity will be prohibited during periods when the roads and trails are muddy. Should your arguments at the meeting prove unpersuasive, you expect the group will try to block the proposed change with a lawsuit.

You come to the meeting prepared to defend the proposal on environmental grounds, but you are worried about a side issue. This forest supports several other types of recreation and a majority of recreation users come from out of state, which is fine with local merchants, but a sore spot with other local residents. You suspect a majority of the snowmobilers will also be from out of state, and you have a good answer should someone object. You can remind them that the forest is a *national* resource, set aside for the welfare of *all* the people and supported by out-of-state, as well as in-state, taxpayers. However, you do not expect this question to come up at the meeting since the group's leaders usually focus most of their attention on environmental issues. Should you refute an objection which hasn't occurred to them? (By the way, this process of preparing an audience for an objection they may hear later is sometimes called *inoculation* – for obvious reasons.)

Suppose you know several members of the environmental group also belong to a local trout fishing club, which provides volunteer labor to help you keep trout streams in good condition. The club, in the past, has stringently objected to out-of-state fishermen invading *their* streams and several trout club members own snowmobiles. Knowing all this, you suspect the issue of out-of-state snowmobilers will come up in a trout club meeting and get carried via the rumor circuit to the chief environmentalists. While the out-of-state issue is logically a minor one for the environmental group, the emotions it generates could help propel them toward a lawsuit.

Under the circumstances, the meeting would be a good place to casually mention the concern about out-of-staters and explain why fairness requires the forest to be open to all. That way, if the issue comes up later when you are not present, people will already have the ready-to-use rebuttal you supplied them with.

6. SUPPORTING POINTS: Look at your brainstorm sheet, your main point, and your list of objections. Pick three or four major supporting points and list each one on a separate sheet of paper.

From the material you have generated and gathered, select a few important points which support your main theme. You may want to circle them with a contrasting color on your mind-map.

7. SUPPORT: Take the sheet for your first supporting point. List all the examples, statistics, anecdotes, analogies, explanations, and other supporting elements you might use. Do the same for the other supporting points.

Organize the remaining material (minor points, quotes, anecdotes, examples, statistics, stories, jokes) under these supporting points. You should make a list or draw a mind-map for each point. Discard anything which doesn't fit. You are now ready to organize the entire speech.

8. OUTLINE: Select from your worksheets those points you wish to use in the speech. Put the points in logical order and construct a concise outline of the body of your speech.

Aristotle also wrote the book on organizing a speech, and most speakers for over 2300 years have followed his lead. That isn't surprising, since his pattern is exceedingly simple. Aristotle said every speech should have three parts:

A beginning,

a middle,

and an end.

When I first heard that, I decided being a Profound Philosopher must be an easy job – just sit around, think up obvious stuff like beginning-middle-end, and say it profoundly. Actually, Aristotle was talking about the same parts of a speech which we call introduction, body, and conclusion.

At first glance, this pattern seems so obvious it is almost absurd to mention it, but many speeches fail by neglecting the obvious. Aristotle said speeches commonly fail because they lack one of the three parts or the parts are not in the right proportion to each other. Have you ever heard a speech which seemed to start from nowhere? Suddenly the speaker was talking and you didn't know who she was or what she was talking about. Aristotle would call that a speech without a beginning. The speaker did not prepare anyone for the body of the speech.

Don't make the mistake of a business association which I heard about in Denver recently. Because times were hard, they couldn't afford a professional speaker, so they hired the treasurer's son-in-law, who lived in Wyoming and was willing to come if the association would buy his plane ticket so he could see the big city. A reporter covering the convention met one of the members coming out of the banquet room.

> *"Has the speaker started yet?"*
> *"Oh yeah, he's been talking half an hour."*
> *"What's he talking about?"*
> *"I don't know. He hasn't said."*

That's what Aristotle was talking about.

Or, what about the speaker you heard who seemed to stop in the middle. You were listening to the speech when suddenly the guy just stopped and sat down. That was a speech without an end – no wrap-up.

Even if a speech has all three parts, it may fail because the parts are not the right length. A speaker can spend too much time in an introduction (setting the stage, giving background information) and lack the time in the body to develop and support the major points. Or a speaker can have a conclusion that is a real barn-burner, complete with ringing calls to action, but have little of substance in the body of the speech. The audience, justifiably, will see no reason to act.

A good rule of thumb is to limit the introduction to 10% to 20% of your total allotted time; also limit the conclusion to 10% to 20%, which leaves 60% to 80% for the body. For longer speeches, the relative time for the introduction and conclusion should shrink. I sometimes teach five-day workshops; if the introduction took 20% of the total time, it would consume the entire first day.

Once you have selected and sorted the material for the speech, organize it into a logical order.

The Standard Pattern

The Standard Pattern is the standard because it is used more than any other. You should use this pattern whenever you are speaking to a group which is favorably inclined toward your position or, at worst, neutral. Because audiences have been listening to speeches with a clear beginning, middle, and end for over 2300 years, they have developed a fairly definite set of expectations. Unless you have a very good reason not to, you should organize your speech to fit those expectations.

Introduction: The audience expects to learn certain things at the beginning of a speech, either from the speaker or from the person who introduces the speaker. They want to know:

The speaker's name

Something about the speaker

The topic

Why they should be interested in the topic

How the speech will be organized

Any necessary background on the topic

In some cases you need to add an attention step to the front of this list. In other cases (a down-to-earth staff meeting) you can simply begin by stating your name and organization.

In deciding what to say about yourself, stick to information that will help you succeed with the speech. Remember what Aristotle said: The audience must believe you are smart enough to know the truth, honest enough to tell the truth, and unselfish enough to have their best interest at heart. You don't have to accomplish all of that in the introduction, but you should establish your right to speak on the subject by explaining your connections with it. An average audience member will more easily believe someone who is smart and well-mannered – just like himself!

The introduction is a good place to introduce similarities and connections between yourself and the audience. For most people that means the introduction will change anytime the audience changes. If I am speaking in Oklahoma, I mention that I grew up on the west side of Oklahoma City. If I am speaking in Texas, I skip the west side of Oklahoma City and instead explain how I went to college and graduate school in Texas. In Louisiana, I say I was born in Shreveport; in Illinois, I mention the four years I worked in Peoria. The situation will dictate how much the audience wants to know, but they will always want to know something, so you seem to be a person they know, instead of just another face.

If someone else will introduce you, both of you need to agree on who will say what. Often, the introduction duty falls on someone who is not a good speaker. In those cases, letting the introducer "wing it" is an invitation to disaster. Since you often can't tell beforehand how good the introducer is, the safest coordination method is to type an outline and also type word-for-word what you want the introducer to say. A person experienced at introductions can take your outline and improvise. Someone less accomplished can just read the introduction. It may sound canned, but at least the audience will get the right information. Always type at least two copies, one to send in advance and one to bring with you in case the first copy gets lost. If the moderator does miss something essential, despite your efforts, you have little choice but to work it into your remarks somehow.

With some careful planning, you may be able to use the moderator's introduction to set up something in your speech, the first joke, perhaps. When my dad was an electric utility executive giving speeches around the Southwest, he repeatedly played on the fact he was from a small Oklahoma town named Poteau ("Poe-toe"). Dad would get the moderator to mention his hometown, and then he would warm up the audience with one or another of his Poteau jokes. ("People keep asking how I got started with the electric company. When I was growing up in Poteau, there were only two places to get a job, the electric company district office and the coal mines. Those that wanted to work hard got a job in the mines.")

Explaining how the speech will be organized is a matter of getting your audience attuned to what is to come, so they will recognize important information when it comes up in the body. This can be accomplished in various ways. The simplest is to put up a slide with a bare-bones outline and mention each of your major supporting points. In the standard pattern there is little point in surprising the audience. Normally, you should tell them up front where the whole speech is leading.

Body: The audience expects you to stick to your theme and arrange your sub-topics in some logical order. Any arrangement that makes sense to you will probably make sense to them. Some typical patterns include:

Chronological – beginning to end, present to past, a typical day in the life of . . . When dates and events are important, this pattern works well.

Spatial – top to bottom, east to west, inside to outside, left to right, front to back, clockwise from the top, etc. This pattern works well when describing physical objects or layouts.

Cause and Effect – either working forward from the initial cause or working backward from the final effect. Investigation reports frequently employ this pattern.

Classification – small to large, conventional to unconventional, useless to practical, expensive to cheap.

Dramatic – trivial to important.

Combination – Several patterns used together. The chronological pattern is frequently combined with cause and effect.

As you will see, this oversight by a maintenance crew on August 12th contributed to the bearing breakdown on September 3rd. Since no corrective action was taken when the problem was discovered on September 5th, the bearing disintegrated on September 7th causing an unscheduled shutdown.

Whatever arrangement you choose, you need to take pains to ensure the audience always knows where you are in the pattern. You may want to put your outline slide back up at intervals, and you certainly want to have a solid transition between each pair of major points. ("We have just seen how the new computer network will affect the office routine, but the effects on the production line will be even more dramatic.") A good transition does two things: it signals the audience that you are moving from one point to the next, and it explains the relationship between the points.

Conclusion: The end can be simple or elaborate. The audience only expects two things: a review of the main point and major supporting points, and a clear signal that the speech is over. If you asked a rhetorical question to gain attention at the beginning, the ending is a good place to answer it. Whatever you do, the final sentence needs to have a definite ring of finality.

While at Air Force Officer Training School in 1968, I learned a military briefing always ends with "Sir, (or "gentlemen") that concludes my briefing. Are there any questions." Air Force briefers are no longer limited to that fixed closing, and most of them realize "sir" will not sit well with a senior female officer, yet that stock sentence is still useful. It makes a good closing for a brief, straightforward, matter-of-fact presentation.

The Late-Breaking Curve Pattern

If your audience is likely to be hostile to your ideas, you may encounter problems with the standard pattern. Imagine a devoted pro-choice advocate with a chance to address a pro-life crowd (or vice versa). Following the standard pattern, a speaker would tell the audience the main point during the introduction. But as soon as this speaker announces the main point, people will decide the whole idea is ridiculous (or pernicious) and tune out the rest of the speech. To cope with this problem, try the Late-Breaking Curve, sometimes known as the Scientific Pattern or the Problem-Solution Pattern.

The basic idea is to delay announcing your conclusion until the evidence is already on the table and the conclusion is inescapable. You may have seen this technique in action in a TV courtroom drama. The lawyer leads a reluctant witness through a series of questions about the facts and, only after the facts are firmly established, confronts the witness with the only possible conclusion.

Another virtue of this pattern is that it lets the audience feel they are participating in solving the problem, since you lead them through the intermediate steps.

Introduction: Use the standard introduction, but don't reveal your thesis. Take particular care in establishing your own credibility. You must appear utterly objective.

Body: First, define the problem or the question. What is driving the audience to the point of decision? Second, discuss the evidence. What has caused the problem? Why did the question arise? What criteria must the answer or solution satisfy? List all possible solutions or answers. Discuss each undesirable solution or answer in turn, carefully explaining what makes them unworkable or undesirable. Discuss the best solution or answer, explaining why it will work better than the others. Explain the results of the best solution. What can we expect to happen after it is implemented?

Conclusion: Review your chain of reasoning. Remind the audience why a solution or answer must be found. Review the various inferior solutions and why they were discarded. Show the audience they have no choice. Unpopular though it is, your conclusion is inescapable; they have no viable alternative. Conclude by calling for action.

The King Speech: I once heard this pattern used by a master. In the spring of 1966, Martin Luther King, Jr. spoke in Dallas, Texas, on the campus of Southern Methodist University. The city authorities were so worried about possible violence they requested the newspapers to withhold all advance publicity, which they did. I learned about the speech only because members of the student senate went to all the scheduled classes that morning to announce it.

In the packed auditorium, tension was high. Most of the audience sat with arms folded at chest level, glaring straight ahead. After Dr. King was introduced, he began speaking very slowly and quietly:

> *I would like to share with you some of the things we have in common in our American heritage.*

For 45 minutes he recounted stories from American history, some familiar, others not. Here was no dramatic orator with thunder in his voice, only a man talking slowly and earnestly about Americans struggling to build a great nation.

After 45 minutes he changed direction:

> *But sometimes things were not as fair as they might have been.*

He continued telling stories, but these were stories of oppression and injustice, such as the Indians' Trail of Tears. As the subject matter changed, so did his delivery. He was speaking faster with a hint of force behind the words, and carrying the audience with him.

After 20 minutes of these stories, he began building to the thundering rhetoric that made him famous. Injustice must be stopped, and we had the power to stop it.

> *People ask, why are you in such a hurry? Don't you*

realize time is on your side? I say, time is not on our side. Time is neutral! We can either use time or have it used against us!

A 5-minute call to action brought the audience to their feet in a standing ovation – the same audience which had greeted him with crossed arms and glares. He had employed the late-breaking curve in a grand style. Had he begun as he ended, with a ringing condemnation of injustice and a call to action, he would have failed, as 90% of the audience tuned him out. Instead, he spent 45 minutes building a common bond with the audience, then 20 minutes laying out the evidence of injustice, and the last 15 minutes summing up the evidence and calling for action.

The late-breaking curve pattern comes with no guarantee. Changing the minds and hearts of an audience dead-set against you is a difficult task under any circumstances. But sometimes the late-breaking curve will work. If it doesn't, nothing else would have worked, either.

The Madison Avenue Pattern

One of the staples of the black and white TV era was the Basic Detergent Commercial. Audiences endured many variations, but the basic version of the Basic Detergent Commercial went like this:

A pretty housewife with frazzled hair is moodily hanging sheets [or perhaps shirts, never undergarments] on her clothes-line.

VOICE OVER: (Mellifluous male voice) *Do you have the washday blues?*

The housewife stares over the fence where her neighbor, who is absolutely beautiful with every hair in place, is also hanging out laundry. Her sheets are snowy white. [Relatively speaking. Remember we are seeing this on a gray screen.] The housewife sighs heavily.

VOICE OVER: *Is your best friend's laundry always cleaner and brighter than yours?*

HOUSEWIFE: *Marge, how do you get your white things so white?*

NEIGHBOR: *I thought you knew, Mildred, I started using Flash.*

CUT TO: The housewife, eyes wide with astonishment, is pulling snowy white sheets out of her washer.

VOICE OVER: *With Flash you can have the cleanest clothes anywhere – in a flash!*

CUT TO: The housewife, smug and beautiful with every hair in place, hangs snowy white sheets on her line while the new neighbor on the other side stares with unconcealed envy.

VOICE OVER: *Imagine how you will feel when your friends come to **you** with **their** washday blues.*

CUT TO: The housewife, beaming, gives the detergent box an affectionate hug.

VOICE OVER: *Don't delay! Get Flash today!*

This cathode-ray classic illustrates what I like to call the Madison Avenue Pattern. Sales people call it the Motivated Sequence, while others call it the Hard Sell Approach. Those names should warn you that you should use this pattern judiciously; it backfires easily.

The pattern draws mixed reviews because it relies more on emotions than logic. As the old lawyer said to the young lawyer:

When the law is on your side, pound on the law. When the evidence is on your side, pound on the evidence. When neither is on your side, pound on the table.

Many speakers become distinctly uncomfortable when asked to play on the emotions of the audience. If you feel a bit squeamish when an emotional appeal is called for, remind yourself of Aristotle's observation. People cannot be convinced unless they are in the right frame of mind. Properly used, emotion does not substitute for logic, but it can change the mood of an audience to make them receptive to logic. As used in advertising, the Madison Avenue Pattern has five steps:

Arouse – (*Do you have the washday blues?*) This step is designed to grab attention by connecting to some need the prospect has, such as the need to feel competent and proud of the family laundry.

Dissatisfy – (*Is your best friend's laundry always cleaner and brighter than yours?*) Create dissatisfaction or make the prospect aware of pre-existing dissatisfaction. No one will change as long as they are happy with the status quo.

Gratify – (*With Flash you can have the cleanest clothes anywhere – in a flash!*) Offer the prospect a way out, something to satisfy the longings created in the previous step.

Picture – (*Imagine how you will feel when your friends come to you with their washday blues.*) Get the prospect to visualize the happy scene when these wants are satisfied.

Move – (*Don't delay! Get Flash today!*) The other steps count for nothing unless the prospect can be moved to action.

In a sales presentation, these five steps can be the basis of your outline. In other types of speeches, they are likely to be modified. Suppose you are speaking to the Chamber of Commerce, trying to line up support for a private summer job training consortium. You could arouse the audience with questions ("How many of you have hired office workers in their teens and twenties and then found out they couldn't type, couldn't spell, couldn't file, and sometimes couldn't read?") Or you could have them imagine a scene:

> *You've hired this guy who doesn't know how to do anything. You try him on filing, but he doesn't know the alphabet, so you ask him to copy a letter and he says, "So, how am I supposed to do that?" You show him and he says, "Hey, you understand this stuff. Why don't you do it yourself?" Then he disappears for a couple of days. When you ask him why, he says, "I couldn't help it; the guy who gives me a ride got picked up."*

With everyone **aroused**, you get them to focus on their **dissatisfaction** with the status quo.

> *How many of you have hired someone in the last five years who lacked basic work skills? How much did you have to spend just to equip them with basic skills? How many of you sell to consumers in the local area? How much more could you sell if the unskilled, unemployed people had jobs?*

As the audience frustration level peaks, you can **gratify** their desire for a change.

> *Our program (which is modeled on successful programs*

in other cities) will take kids without job skills, train them in job responsibilities, and place them in subsidized jobs. Because we are picking up their salaries, you can afford to hire them and provide a little on-the-job training. They have to keep working hard because we monitor their progress. Best of all, after a kid has been in the program a couple of years, the community gets a productive worker, a taxpayer, and a consumer with money in his pocket.

You then take them a step beyond understanding by getting them to **visualize** the benefits.

Imagine this: three years from now you hire one of our graduates to take orders by phone and sort the mail. Her third day on the job, the annual January blizzard hits; you are stranded, but somehow this new kid gets in to work. She is the only one there, so she calls your house to see if you are all right, then holds down the fort until the snow plows can clear the streets for everyone else. When you finally get there after lunch, she shows you the twelve orders she has taken on the phone and entered in the computer. Some of the formatting is screwy, but all the vital data is there. And this is a kid who grew up in one of those projects on the west side of town!

With the emotional current flowing in your direction, you **move** the audience before the mood shifts.

I'm passing around two sheets. Sign up on this yellow one if you are willing to hire one or more trainees for the summer. Remember we pick up the salary. Sign on the green sheet to become a corporate sponsor. Every dollar you contribute is matched two to one by the government.

Keep the Pattern Simple

Whichever pattern you use, remember to keep the basic structure simple. Complexity in any form threatens a speaker's success. If you must communicate something complex, put it in writing. Readers can comprehend complex material because they read at their own pace, can stop and look up words, if necessary, and can reread any paragraph which is confusing. Listeners do none of that. And, while listeners in conversation can stop the talker and request clarification, audience members are usually reluctant to stop a speech.

On the plus side, speaking offers two advantages over writing: increased interaction with the audience, and increased impact. But without simplicity, impact is lost. The greatest of all American speakers was Abraham Lincoln (despite his shrill voice and ungainly appearance). Lincoln was not born with the skills of a master persuader; he had to learn them through hard study, as we all do.

One of the lessons Lincoln taught himself was the power of simplicity. Consider this passage from an early speech when he seemed to worship ornate elaboration:

> *Their's was the task (and nobly they performed it) to possess themselves, and through themselves, us, of this goodly land; and to uprear upon its hills and its valleys, a political edifice of liberty and equal rights; 'tis ours only, to transmit these, the former, unprofaned by the foot of an invader; the latter, undecayed by the lapse of time, and untorn by usurpation – to the latest generation that fate shall permit the world to know.[15]*

This passage, spoken in 1838, is so artfully complex it is difficult to decipher even in print. Twenty-five years later, when he was asked to make some "Dedicatory Remarks" for the national cemetery at Gettysburg, he returned to the same concepts. But now he knew that simplicity brings power.

> *. . . our fathers brought forth on this continent, a new nation conceived in Liberty, and dedicated to the proposition that all men are created equal.*
> *. . . It is rather for us to be here dedicated to the great task remaining before us . . . that government of the people, by the people, for the people, shall not perish from the earth.*

Styles in rhetoric change just as styles in clothing do, but observe the great speeches of any generation and you will find the same principle verified. Simplicity brings power. One contemporary speaker who knows that well is Jesse Jackson. Consider this comment made on a TV interview:

*There are two problems which primarily afflict America
today: too many drugs coming in; too many jobs going out.*

Not everyone who hears a comment like that agrees, but everyone understands, and everyone remembers. Working with few campaign resources beyond his own eloquence, he gained over a thousand delegates for the Democratic National Convention in 1988.

Another speaker who packs power into short phrases is Ross Perot:

I won't spend ten years looking at a ten minute problem.

Whether you agree with their positions or not, remember their method. Simplicity brings power.

Executive Summary

1. Before organizing a speech, you need to determine who the principal decision-makers in the audience will be.

2. Using your analysis of the audience, decide what motivation you can provide. What will audience members gain by doing what you want?

3. Write down in one sentence the most important idea you want the audience to remember.

4. List likely objections and how you will answer them. Decide whether to put each answer in the speech or save it to use in response to a question.

5. From your various lists of ideas, pick three or four major points.

6. Sort your other ideas; under each of your major points put the ideas which support it.

7. Drop ideas you will not use and put the others in a logical order.

8. In the Standard Pattern for a speech, the audience learns in the introduction what the main point of the speech will be. This pattern works well with audiences which are favorably inclined or at least neutral to the speaker's point of view.

9. If the audience is likely to be hostile to the speaker's ideas, the Late-Breaking Curve Pattern is likely to be more effective than the Standard Pattern. In the Late-Breaking Curve Pattern, the speaker sells the audience

on each link in the chain of reasoning and presents them with the conclusion only after they have accepted the evidence which makes the conclusion inescapable.

10. The Madison Avenue Pattern used in TV commercials can be effective in changing the audience's mood. The pattern has five steps:

a. Arouse

b. Dissatisfy

c. Gratify

d. Picture

e. Move

11. Whatever the pattern, keeping it simple will give it more power.

6

Adding Interest: Jokes and Stories

In planning a speech, you need to decide whether to use humor and, if so, where to use it. When properly applied, humor has many advantages. It can help you establish a bond with the audience, defuse criticism, hold interest, and make your main points memorable.

The Connected Joke

Some speakers misuse humor and send the minds of their audience galloping down dead end streets with jokes that are unconnected to anything in the speech. I once heard a college student begin a Bible study thus, "I'm glad to be here today. Did you hear the one about the two rich fleas who bought themselves a dog? Today we are going to look at the Gospel of John." For humor to benefit a speech, it must be linked to the speaker, topic, audience, or occasion.

In my week-long workshop for supervisors, I introduce one point with this story:

> *Betty Lou Matthews and Edgar Hergesheimer were sitting in the back room of the old folks home. Betty Lou turned to Edgar and said, "If you take off all your clothes, I can tell how old you are."*

"Say what?"

"If you take off all your clothes, I can tell how many years and how many months you are old."

He got up, looked around, didn't see anybody, so he took his clothes off. Betty Lou looked him up and down – looked him up and down again. Finally, Edgar said, "Well?"

"You are 84 years and 3 months old."

"Wha???? How'd you know that?!"

"Told me yourself last week."

Then I make this point: Betty Lou got exactly what she wanted because she said exactly what she wanted. We bridge from that idea into distinguishing clear goals (smile at the customers) from fuzzy goals (exhibit a professional attitude). The story makes the point about goals memorable. Days later I can ask,

"Do you remember why Betty Lou at the old folks home got what she wanted?"

"Yeah, she had clear goals."

The requirement to have each joke accomplish something means you won't be able to use some jokes – even some of the funniest. It also means you may find a joke which makes a perfect illustration for a key point, but the joke is old and well-worn. You can still use it, but don't try to pass it off as a fresh joke. Instead, introduce it by saying, "Here's an old story," or "You may have heard this one." With those remarks, you change the audience's expectations. Since they don't expect a fresh joke, they will accept a well-traveled one, as long as it makes your point clearly.

Good Taste

Humor should also be kind (not destructive) and in good taste. You risk your own credibility telling jokes which are vicious or crude. What is in good taste varies with the occasion, of course, but be conservative. Some people who will tell a dirty joke in private are deeply offended hearing the same joke in public. Be very cautious with ethnic, religious, or political jokes unless you are telling them on your own group. (A Catholic will know better than a Protestant where to draw the line with jokes about the Pope.) You remember Betty Lou and Edgar at the old folks home? Let's take another look at that story because it illustrates how to keep risque material acceptable.

> *"If you take off all your clothes, I can tell how old you are."*

This line sets up suspense on two levels. On one level, the imagination of the audience is tantalized. (What will happen after he takes his clothes off?) On the other level, the audience is teased over propriety. (Can the speaker tell this racy story without falling into the pit of vulgarity?) We know the story is racy because the two people are not married to each other. To actually say they are not married would slow down the story; the audience easily picks up the idea from the different last names.

We know the punch line is close when Edgar takes off his clothes, but no description is necessary. The speaker doesn't comment on Edgar's appearance and doesn't mention what parts of him Mary Lou looks at. ("Looks him up and down" is a purposely general description.) In other words, the speaker only drops hints and lets the audience's imagination supply the racy details. The story ends with the punch line, of course, which means nothing else happens between the characters; the audience is left safely within the bounds of conventional morality.

Most jokes are semi-replaceable. If you have one which makes you nervous and you can't tone it down, finding a safe replacement joke may be easier than experimenting with the original to see if it can be made to work safely.

Whenever you can't find a good replacement, you can test the original questionable joke when you rehearse the speech. Assemble a rehearsal audience which is demographically similar to the real audience. Try especially hard to get a close match in age range, ethnic background, and educational level. As you give the speech, watch the reactions. After the speech, ask the audience to comment on the joke. If the rehearsal audience closely resembles the real audience, and the rehearsal audience is not bothered, you can feel fairly secure in using the material.

The importance of staying within the audience's concept of good taste cannot be overemphasized. Jokes which play well to a party audience may not play well to a speech audience, *even if the same people are present.* I have witnessed this irony more than once, yet the only explanation I have heard is that people in a speech audience are more conscious of the attention of those around them. To avoid embarrassment, they stick closer to conventional morality.

In some situations, anything funny will be in bad taste. Several years ago, a woman who was responsible for health and wellness issues for the Rocky Mountain division of a large organization became convinced that rank and file workers were uninformed about the immediate danger of AIDS. From internal sources she knew several managers had died from AIDS-related illnesses and several others had taken early retirement for the same reason. The departure of each of these people had been described euphemistically to protect their privacy, but those euphemisms reinforced the complacency of managers and workers, alike. She asked my advice on a "wake-em-up" speech she intended to deliver at every office in the region. Her main point was that people must take precautions immediately; AIDS was not just a problem in ghettos and the Third World – it was on our doorstep *NOW*. To make her point crystal clear, she intended to hand a condom in its original wrapper to every audience member.

She wanted me to watch her practice before a trial audience and tell her whether the speech would be effective. When I watched the presentation, her information was sobering. To lighten the mood, she made several clever remarks about condoms. In the critique session, she asked me whether handing out condoms was too much. I told her it was one of those rare bits that is like dynamite – if she handled it exactly right, it would be more powerful than anything she could do. If she made a single mistake, it could blow up in her face.

I saw two spots where she risked that explosion. She advocated safe sex, but said nothing about abstinence. For some audience members, she would appear to be advocating promiscuity. Then there was the issue of the jokes. She could put in jokes somewhere else, but by joking about condoms she risked appearing flippant, and she seemed to send a mixed message. (As if to say, "This is a serious issue – well, maybe not that serious.")

She made the changes and gave the speech to another group the next day. This time she said the only sure protection was abstinence, but if people intended on having sex, anyway, they should at least limit the risk. Then she handed out condoms to a somber-looking crowd. The effect was dynamite!

Who Laughs at What?

Be sure to keep your audience's frame of reference in mind. That joke about a heifer caught in a silo, which had them rolling in the aisles at the local farmers cooperative, may bring only puzzled frowns when you try it on the Jaycees. ("What's a heifer?") A good audience analysis should give you an idea of the sorts of things that are likely to work, but there is no substitute for actual testing.

Play To Your Strengths

The secret to making material funny is to play within your own capabilities. There are countless funny people in this world, but they are funny in different ways. Bob Hope's best material is a string of rapid-fire one-liners, while Bill Cosby tells, and sometimes acts out, short character sketches. It is difficult to imagine either of them working with the other's material. Find out what you do best. If you are good at telling jokes, do that. If you are good at puns, work some in. If you do accents, try one on. If you play to your strengths, the audience need not discover your weaknesses.

Test everything. Don't tell a joke for the first time in a speech. Working up a humorous speech is like editing a film: you want to leave the bad parts on the cutting-room floor. Try things out and drop the parts that don't work.

If You Can't Tell a Joke

We have seen that Bob Hope and Bill Cosby are both immensely successful comedians, but what they do to be funny is radically different. Most of us are like that. In looking for funny material, we concentrate on the style of joke we tell best.

However, some people seem to have trouble with all types of jokes. It should be obvious that you should refrain from using jokes if you don't tell them well. In fact, jokes are one exception to the rule about not memorizing a speech. Memorizing a joke is far better than blowing the punch line.

You may find it easier to tell a humorous anecdote from real life instead of a joke. Easier, because you don't need to embellish it – you simply tell the story. Anecdotes rarely require perfect timing, and they also carry a greater sense of reality than jokes. If the anecdote is a good one, you have probably polished your technique by telling it often.

I sometimes teach a workshop on Dealing With Difficult People. One type of difficult person I encountered occasionally while in the Air Force was the Rule-Bound Robot. To illustrate how this person operates, I tell this story:

> *In 1987 I was playing basketball when I ruptured the Achilles tendon on my left foot. The doctor said I would have*

been better off breaking a bone, and he was right. I spent six weeks in a full-leg cast, another six weeks in a half-leg cast, and four months in a brace.

After I had the first cast a month, my daughter sprained her ankle – and they put her in a cast. By chance, she was scheduled to get her cast off the same day I was scheduled to switch from the full- to the half-cast. She was working as a camp counselor, so, with my one good foot, I drove from Dayton, Ohio, to Stony Lake, Michigan, to pick her up, then back to the Air Force hospital at Dayton.

Not being content to have people sign her cast, she had decorated it with beads and feathers on a leather thong. I parked close to the hospital, Kate took off the cast decorations, and together we hobbled through the hospital building.

If you have ever had a non-weight-bearing cast, you know how painful crutches are. Every second step you support 100% of your body weight on your armpits. Not only do your armpits ache; the rubber pads rub the skin off your ribs. For some reason, the Air Force put the orthopedic ward on the third floor and on the opposite side of the building from the parking lot. But, eventually, we made it.

While I was waiting for an orderly to start sawing, I heard a page: "Major Harlan, please come to the front desk. Major Harlan, please come to the front desk." I asked the orderly if I could call the front desk, but he said, "That's O.K., sir, I'll go see what they want."

Five minutes later the orderly called me on the phone. "Sir, there's a civilian policeman from the base here. He says you have to come down and move your car immediately!"

"Why?"

"He says you are parking in a handicapped zone without a handicapped sticker."

"That's a long walk on crutches."

"I know, sir, that's why I told him we had your cast halfway off. He said to move the car as soon as we are through. In the meantime, he's going to give you a ticket."

The orderly came back and started sawing on my cast; then we heard another page, "Major Harlan, please come to the front desk . . ." The orderly jumped up: "It's O.K. – I'll go talk to him." Five minutes later the phone rang.

"Sir, the policeman wants to arrest you for contraband in your car."

"What??"

"Yes, sir. He said you have game bird feathers on your dash. Under the Migratory Bird Treaty Act, you can get six months in jail and a $10,000 fine."

"What for?"

"Except for Indians, it's illegal to transport game bird feathers across state lines without a permit. He wants to know what kind of feathers these are, where you got them, where you have transported them, and what you intend to do with them."

I said, "Listen closely, so you can repeat this. These are blue heron feathers, which my daughter picked up on the ground beside Stony Lake in Michigan. She did no harm to any blue heron, living or dead. I have transported them from Stony Lake to here, and I intend to keep them because I am part Cherokee!"

After a pause, "Sir, he says it's all right about the feathers, but he's giving you a ticket for the handicapped zone."

This story is simultaneously the best-rehearsed and the freshest piece of material in that program. The best-rehearsed, because I have told it innumerable times to family members and friends. The freshest, because no one in a typical audience has heard it before. I have never found a joke that no one in the audience knew.

Borrowing Anecdotes

Be cautious, however, about borrowing anecdotes from other speakers. If you tell a story from your life, it will sound fresh; if you borrow one, the audience may be hearing it for the fourteenth time. For the same reason, as you develop more speeches, you should try to work new stories into each one rather than using the same stories over and over. Someone who hears you once and makes a special effort to hear you on another topic will feel cheated if you drag out the same stories.

If you do borrow an anecdote which happened to someone else, you must give credit (*Janet Spivey told me about the time she was on the beach and lost her car keys . . .*). Never tell a story which happened to someone else as if it happened to you. Jokes are an exception; a speaker can begin a joke as if it were a personal experience. The fanciful style associated with jokes will tipoff the audience that this particular story is not a personal experience.

Why you should avoid telling a story which happened to someone else as if it happened to you is not clear to all public speakers. Some speakers, especially older ones, are likely to see no harm in it. A few of the highly successful public speakers I have heard have told as personal experiences stories for which I knew the source. Although this practice is fairly widespread, standards are changing. The same people who hold today's politicians to tougher standards than their parents did, are applying the same rules to the rest of us who speak in public.

The public used to allow all speakers a certain amount of rhetorical freedom, letting them restructure material to make it more vivid or more personal. Audiences today are less tolerant on this point, and I believe tomorrow's audiences will be even stricter. The problem, from the standpoint of the audience, is that a speaker who pretends he had an experience when he didn't, raises questions throughout the speech. Is he pretending to know the facts, as well?

Even if you never convert other material into personal experiences, you can get put in a jam by other people who do. Consider this story:

> *My friend John Doe told me he was walking on the beach at (location) one evening when he saw a guy picking up starfish which were stranded when the tide went out. If they didn't get back in the water, they would die. So every time this guy found a stranded starfish he would throw it as far out in the ocean as possible. John couldn't understand it, so he went up to the guy and said,*
>
> *"Don't you realize there are literally millions of starfish dying every day on beaches around the world. Here you are throwing them back one by one. What difference can that possibly make?"*
>
> *The guy picked up another starfish and pitched it as far out in the ocean as he could. "Made a difference to that starfish."*

From a speaker's standpoint, this story looks like pure gold: it's short; it's easy to visualize; and it makes one important point so clearly that no comment is required. Unfortunately, it may turn out to be fool's gold. In the last two years I have heard audio tapes of two speakers telling this story. The two versions of the story were virtually identical except that each of the speakers named a different John Doe. Each of them claimed to have heard the story from the man it happened to, but they did not agree on who that was. Curiously, each of the John Does was also a speaker.

I suppose it is possible that on a beach, somewhere, some man is wandering at low tide pitching starfish in the ocean. And it is also possible that this hurler of starfish keeps bumping into public speakers, each of whom asks him the same question. All of that is possible, but it reminds me of the defense college students sometimes give for plagiarism. The student just happened to have the same ideas as Robert Frost while walking through snowy woods one evening.

More than likely, some speaker invented the starfish story, and other speakers have been borrowing and adapting it ever since. If you also borrow it, you may tell it to someone who just heard a purportedly authentic version from someone else the day before.

So what can you do with a useful story like this one when its ancestry is uncertain? Either track down the source or convert it to a hypothetical story. Tracking down the source may lead you to conclude the story is apocryphal; it never actually happened to anyone. In that case, you can still convert it to a hypothetical story. Here's an example of how to do it:

> *Imagine your organization sends you out to Santa Maria, California, on a special project. The first day you drive down to the beach and find it almost deserted because the weather has turned chilly and windy.*
>
> *Then you notice one guy out there picking up things and throwing them in the ocean. You are curious, so you walk over to him.*
>
> . . .
>
> *"What difference could it possibly make?"*
> *You watch him pick up one more starfish, standed by the tide, and pitch it as far as he can.*
> *"Made a difference to that starfish."*

Another way to convert a story to hypothetical is to detach it from all details of time and place:

> *A skeptic walked down to the beach one day and saw a*

> *philosopher picking up starfish from the beach and throwing them in the ocean. He asked why, and the philosopher explained that starfish get stranded when the tide goes out and will die unless someone puts them back in the water.*
>
> *"But there are millions of starfish dying on beaches around the world. You can't possibly save more than a couple of dozen. What difference can you make?"*
>
> *The philosopher threw another starfish as far as he could. "I made a difference to that starfish."*

By converting the story to hypothetical, you relinquish any claim that it actually happened, but you gain the freedom to mold it according to your needs.

Finding Material

If you are going to give after-dinner speeches, funny material is a must. But even if you stick to matter-of-fact business speaking, you will find humor useful. A funny story can defuse hostility, make a point memorable, or relieve some of the physical stress on a committee that has been sitting too long. As the occasions for you to give a speech, briefing, or presentation increase, so does the need for funny material. Your persuasiveness will erode if you keep telling the same stories over and over.

I mentioned earlier in this chapter that the funny anecdotes you recall and tell for family and friends are among the best sources for material. Providing you have enough family stories and you are adept at connecting them to points in a speech, you may not need another source. However, most of us find the supply of family lore is insufficient to cover all our needs. The basic sources for usable stories, anecdotes, and jokes are these:

1. You stumble into something interesting or funny.

2. You hear someone else tell a joke you can adapt.

3. You read jokes, stories, or anecdotes.

4. You invent what you need.

You Stumble Into Something

Near an intersection on a route I sometimes drive in Aurora, Colorado, are two signs. The first says "NO LEFT TURN." Behind it is another, which says "LEFT LANE MUST TURN LEFT." If I ever need a slide illustrating bureaucratic confusion, I know where to shoot it.

In my proofreading workshop, I put on the screen part of a resume sent to me by a job hunter who said she was an "expert in commication,"[sic] followed by one from a secretary who "always gets things wright."[sic] After seeing those quotes, a participant in one of the workshops told me of a honky-tonk in his hometown with this sign:

Nude   Food
Dancing Cocktails

When I was teaching proofreading in Australia, I came across a delightful newspaper column, *When Words Fail* by Patricia and Frank Horner. That day they were concentrating on unintended puns from various newspapers. They found that orange juice concentrate was "flooding the market" and "frivolous underwear has taken off" under the influence of pop singers.

All of these are useful bits because they have an obvious connection with proofreading, and they were not hard to find. All I had to do was stay alert for possible material as I went about my daily business.

Interaction with other people can be a rich source of material. Several years ago, my wife and I went with our friends, Bob and Pat Ove, to a symphony concert featuring works by Tchaikovsky. After the concert we went to an almost deserted cafe in downtown Denver.

As Bob and Pat discussed Tchaikovsky, they attracted the attention of a man sitting at a booth across the aisle. Suddenly, he joined in, "You know who wrote more opuses than Tchaikovsky?"

We all turned to look and saw a man in his thirties wearing a blue velvet shirt, faded jeans, and penny-loafers sans socks. He had a back pack on the seat beside him and had hair halfway down his back. After a moment, Bob said, "who wrote more than Tchaikovsky?"

"Yeah, it was two guys named Herman and Yugoslavsky."

"Yugoslavsky? Was he Yugoslavian?"

With our full attention on him, this expert in blue velvet stood up. "Yugoslavian, Hungarian, one of those. And not only that, Rodgers and Hammerstein did not write Oklahoma! There was this Russian couple wrote it, and Rodgers and Hammerstein took all the credit – See, the way I know all this is I flew in from L.A. today, and I'm going up to Boulder, to the University of Colorado to get a master's in music history." As his lecture picked up speed, he crossed to our table where he saw Bob's clerical collar. "You're a minister!"

"Yes."

"I was going to be a minister, but I was too busy making porno movies."

Bob almost jumped out of his seat – "You too! I USED TO MAKE PORN FLICKS BEFORE I BECAME A MINISTER!"

Material like this is priceless – if you can capture it. I know this event happened exactly as I have told it here because I wrote down all the details as soon as I got home. I now use this illustration in my program on Dealing With Difficult People to demonstrate behavior typical of a Foremost Phony, someone who talks like an expert, but isn't.

To capitalize on material you stumble into, you need a system for capturing and preserving it. Whenever you observe something that is potentially useful, make notes about it and file the notes, either in one file marked "Illustrations" or in several files arranged by topic.

You Hear Someone Else Tell a Joke You Can Adapt

As mentioned earlier, other speakers' experiences are not a good source of material; your own experiences are much better. But other speakers' jokes are fair game, as are the jokes you hear in conversation. Jokes are very pliable, which makes them easy to adapt to your purposes. Suppose you hear this joke told at a convention:

> *One thing I love about our association president is how he never lets anything interfere with his golf game. Frank, did you tell them about that forty-foot putt yesterday? I saw it. He only missed the clown's mouth by this much.*

You can use this joke with minimal variations anytime you speak to a group with a prominent leader who plays golf and can take a joke. As explained above, each joke in a speech needs to serve some definite purpose. This one helps you bond with the audience by sharing their amusement at the foibles of one group member. Depending on your speech topic, it can reinforce other points:

> *You don't have to be an Olympic athlete to benefit from*

exercise. That reminds me of yesterday's golf game. Frank, did you tell them . . .

You don't pick up a new skill by watching it on TV. Whether we are talking about telemarketing, proposal writing, or golf, you have to keep practicing. Take our chairman, for instance. With all the things going on here yesterday, he still found time to work in a round of golf. Frank, did you tell them . . .

It's easy to blow things out of proportion. Did any of you hear Frank talking about his forty-foot putt yesterday. I saw it. He only missed . . .

With some restructuring, the same joke can be told on yourself. Self-deprecating humor is one of the best ways of connecting with an audience.

I like to keep my life in balance, so yesterday I took some time off to play a little golf. Now, you may not believe this, but I made this incredible forty-foot putt. It only missed the clown's mouth by this much.

When you hear a joke which fits your style of humor, scribble down the basic idea and put it in your Illustrations file.

You Read Jokes, Stories, or Anecdotes

When you need more material in a hurry, you may have a hard time arranging to hear more jokes, but the number you can read is limited only by your schedule. Joke anthologies abound, but I find the typical anthology material hard to adapt. An exception is *Podium Humor*[16] by former presidential speech-writer James C. Humes. Some of his material is easy to adapt and some of it will work as is. Consider this string of one-liners designed to open a speech to a farm group:

I appreciate your welcome. As the cow said to the farmer one winter morning, "Thank you for a warm hand."
Really, we farmers need all the help we can get. As Pope John, whose own roots were in the soil, once said, "People go

to ruin in three ways -- women, gambling, and farming. My family chose the slowest one.''

Actually, if you work hard and long enough on a farm, you can make a fortune – that is, if you strike oil.

My ambition, though, is to be one of those gentlemen farmers. That's one who has time to read all the government literature on farming.[17]

If I had to talk to a farm group on short notice, I would grab this bit to start with. Later, if I had time to tinker, I could work in some local material, but if I had to have something quick, these one-liners would work without modification.

Another excellent source for both anecdotes and jokes is the *Reader's Digest*. Their material is always pithy and appeals to a wide range of audiences. I sometimes take a couple of issues with me on an airplane; I tear out the pages with jokes and stories, circle the material I can use, and file the pages with the appropriate subject when I get home.

You Invent What You Need

Where do jokes come from? Most people, who only repeat the jokes they hear, don't give much thought to that question. Every joke, no matter how many times it has been retold, was invented by someone. Somebody, somewhere, told it for the first time. Professional comics and their writers account for only a fraction of the total. Most jokes were created by ordinary people who like to amuse their friends. You and I can use the same process to invent funny speech material. The process has four steps:

1. Determine the purpose of the joke.

2. Generate possibilities.

3. Refine the best possibility.

4. Test the joke on others.

Let's look at each step in turn.

Determine the purpose of the joke. One purpose of every joke is to create enjoyment. We tell jokes to get people to laugh. But in a speech, each joke must accomplish something more. We use a joke to loosen people up and introduce the subject. For instance, let's suppose you are running an international shipping business. You have been invited to speak about "The Global Economy" at a luncheon sponsored by a professional women's club. You need some funny material to introduce the idea that "we are all coming together, but we are in for rough times ahead."

Generate possibilities. People who need volumes of funny material often work in groups to generate it by brainstorming. Whether you work alone or in a group, it helps to have some sort of outline to spark ideas. Think about the typical patterns familiar jokes fall into:

I've got good news and bad news.

A Protestant minister, a priest, and a rabbi were . . .

The good fairy said, "I'll grant you three wishes."

Two people appeared before St. Peter at the heavenly gates.

Now think about the stereotypes and themes most people believe about the global economy.

America is losing its competitive edge.

Japanese corporations are taking over the world.

Most American corporations have slip-shod customer service.

An astute student of global affairs will realize that most of these stereotypes are only half true. They are useful, nonetheless, because they are broadly based. A joke which plays off these concepts will be recognizable to every audience member.

Now, think of combinations of the joke patterns and the stereotypes. Here's the line of thinking I went through.

The good news about a firm's customer service would be "no complaints." The bad news could be "lots of complaints," but stated that way it is not funny. Maybe the bad news is "no customers." That's funny, partly because "no complaints" and "no customers." are similar in structure.

How can we acknowledge in a joke the fear that the Japanese are taking over everything? Maybe we have two people arrive at the pearly gates 50 years from now.

St. Peter's roster says one of them is the American president, but he only speaks Japanese. So who is the other person, and what does St. Peter say before the president delivers his punch line in Japanese? This line of attack appears to have serious obstacles. To set it up properly will require a long involved story, and the punch line isn't good enough for a long buildup. If the punch line comes quickly, it will be funny. If it arrives slowly, it will be a letdown.

Maybe I can keep the punch line and build a simpler story around it. Suppose someone from the future comes back in a time machine.

Refine the best possibility. After you run out of possibilities, go back and pick the best of the rough jokes and tighten them, so they have the energy and punch of good jokes.

> *The service manager for an American car dealer goes into the dealer's office. "I've got good news and bad news." Dealer says, "What's the good news?" "We haven't had a customer complaint in three weeks." "What's the bad news?" "We haven't had a customer in three weeks."*

> *My wife told me she had a dream last night. Michael J. Fox and Christopher Lloyd picked her up in their time machine and took her 100 years into the future to interview the president of the world. I said, "That's exciting. What's the world like in 100 years?" "I don't know; he only spoke Japanese."*

Test the joke on others. Predicting which jokes will strike an audience as funny can be harder than predicting a horse race. Try out your creations on your family and friends, and, based on their input and your own intuition, keep a joke as is, restructure it, polish it, or drop it.

One-Liners

One-liners are not just shorter versions of the standard joke. They differ in structure and in their relationship to surrounding material. A joke, even a short joke, is basically narrative – it's a story in abbreviated form.

> *I told my mother I was worried about speaking in front of so many people.*
>
> *"Relax," she said. "You don't have to be witty or profound. Just be yourself."*

One-liners are more like a commentary. That's why stand-up comics use so many one-liners. For maximum effectiveness, one-liners should be used in a series, all on the same subject. That way, each laugh builds on the one before. Consider this series by James Humes.

> *As an advertising man, let me say that was a fine introduction. You turned a kernel of fact into a field of corn.*
>
> *Seriously, though, imagination is what makes a great copywriter. If you don't believe me, just read my write-up of my monthly expense account.*
>
> *It doesn't bother me, though; I know that my ulcers react only when I begin to get inhibited by the facts.*
>
> *Really, though, I am proud of my profession. Advertising has made America great, but then you might say advertising makes everything look great.[18]*

This series illustrates another important point. Politicians use one-liners to attack the other party. Standup comics use them to attack practically everybody. The fact that the injured parties are mad is of little consequence. The rest of us speakers are not that lucky; we must pick our targets carefully or the one-liners will destroy all the rapport we have built. As this series illustrates, the safest possible target is the speaker himself.

Conventional jokes can be adapted for different purposes in a speech, but one-liners are typically a warm-up routine near the beginning of a speech. They can be hard to fit in elsewhere.

When Jokes Bomb

At one time or another, every speaker has tried a set of one-liners or a joke that failed. Instead of laughing, the audience just sits and stares. Sometimes the speaker can figure out what went wrong, but she often has no clue. Even if the speaker realizes instantly what the problem is, she still has to somehow get past the dead spot and go on with the speech. By listening carefully to other speakers, you will notice most of them rescue themselves by a clever adlib. Actually, not a true adlib, the comment has been memorized just for such a situation. If you are going to tell jokes or one-liners, prepare for the worst by memorizing one or more of the comments below, or making up your own.

> *My wife told me that story would never work. I see you all side with her.*

> *[Reading off index card] It says here, "wait for laugh."*

> *That's the last joke I buy from [person well-known to audience].*

If you are troubled by the risk involved in telling jokes, listen to the comments made about other speakers. Many are criticized for being too dull – very few for being too funny.

Executive Summary

1. For humor to benefit a speech, it must be linked to the speaker, topic, audience, or occasion.

2. You may find a joke which makes a perfect illustration for a key point, but the joke is old and well-worn. You can still use it if you say, "Here's an old story," or "You may have heard this one."

3. Be especially careful to keep your jokes within the bounds of good taste (as defined by the audience). A stand-up comic can risk offending people; a speaker cannot.

4. Different speakers are funny in different ways. Use material that fits your style.

5. If you can't tell a joke, use anecdotes instead.

6. Audiences today are less accepting of speakers who borrow anecdotes and tell them as first-person experiences. A better strategy is to give credit and tell about the person the anecdote actually happened to.

7. The basic sources for usable stories, anecdotes, and jokes are these:

    a. You stumble into something interesting or funny.

    b. You hear someone else tell a joke you can adapt.

    c. You read jokes, stories, or anecdotes.

    d. You invent what you need.

8.   One-liners differ in concept from short jokes. Jokes are basically narrative – stories in abbreviated form. One-liners are more like a commentary.

9. Use one-liners in a series, all on the same subject.

10. Every speaker who uses humor needs to memorize some stock adlibs to use if a joke bombs.

7

Creating Visual Aids

Giving a speech with visual aids is like doing a striptease: what the audience sees may be good or bad, but, either way, it makes a big impression. Since an audience will judge your speech largely by what they see, you should plan your visual aids carefully. Creating a visual aid can be thought of as a four step process:

Selecting a medium

Designing the images

Producing the finished product

Testing the finished product

Selecting a Medium

In some cases, your choice of a visual aid medium will be dictated. If it is not, you should look at the information in Appendix IV and make an appropriate choice. Factors to consider include:

1. The audience. How many people will be there and what are their expectations?

2. The place. Does it have electricity? Must equipment be transported? Can the room be sufficiently darkened? Can all the audience members see?

3. Dependability of equipment

4. Your budget

5. Available lead time

6. Your purpose

Designing the Images

Once you have chosen the medium, you must design the images which will be shown to the audience. The instructions in this chapter deal only with creating still images, whether 35mm slides, overhead transparencies, LCD displays, or flip charts/flip cards. Producing a video or conventional movie is a complicated process beyond the scope of this work, but books on the subject abound. See your local library.

For convenience, we will use the term *slide* to refer to any image, no matter what the subject matter (chart, outline, cartoon, etc.) and no matter what the medium.

You should be thinking of possible slides at the same time you are planning other aspects of the speech. Visual aids add impact and aid audience retention, so you should be looking for those points in your speech that need to be stressed. And because visual aids can show things that are difficult to explain, you should also be looking for those points where explanations may fail. If you cannot think of a better pattern, you can always use the traditional slide set: an overview slide, a slide for each major point, and a final summary slide.

Once you know what you want to illustrate or emphasize, you are ready to choose the type of slide which will do it best. The paragraphs which follow describe the strengths and weaknesses of each type of slide. Once you know the type of slide you need, scribble a rough draft on a piece of paper. When you have the speech planned, you should also have a stack of scribbled slide drafts to guide you in producing the actual slides.

Text Slides: This could be an outline, a list, or a short quotation or statement. Text slides should always be simplified to the maximum extent possible. If you have a long quotation, consider reading it aloud and putting only the punch line on the slide. You will rarely go wrong with a text slide if you stay within these guidelines:

1. Limit each slide to only one main point. (And the point should be obvious at first glance.)

2. Limit each slide to six lines of text.

3. Limit each line to six words.

4. Use both small case and capital letters.

5. Use blank space to make text stand out.

6. Use the largest possible lettering. On an overhead transparency, letters should be at least a quarter-inch high.

7. Make every letter as bold as possible.

Guidelines 2 and 3 are flexible. If the lines contain only two to four words, you might have eight lines, for instance. If you needed ten words on a line, but only planned three lines, that would also work. Research with audiences has shown that once you get more than 36-40 words on a single image, the audience will not read it. Researchers have also learned that printing with all capitals is hard to read; people can do it, but it slows them down. A few words in caps for emphasis will do no harm, but don't put every word in all caps.

To find a good model for a text slide, you need look no further than your own TV. Television advertising time during the Super Bowl in most years will cost over $700,000 for a 30 second spot. That figure is just for air time; it does not include production costs. Advertisers who spend that kind of money will do everything possible to ensure the ads are effective. By looking closely at TV ads, you will notice some of them incorporate what we are calling a text slide. That is, at one or two spots during the commercial, the screen will have several lines of stationary text. While watching the Winter Olympics in 1988, I saw the following four slides in a one-hour period. In each case, the slide was projected against a solid background.

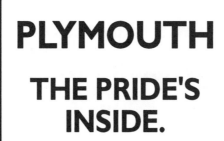

Figure 7-1

More Americans get their news from ABC News than from any other source.

Figure 7-2

"Jennings ... knows the world beat better than anyone."

The Dallas Morning News

Figure 7-3

Timely Advice From
Merrill Lynch

Figure 7-4

Notice that each of these slides is well within the six words/six lines limit and the main point of each is obvious. A speaker who has to explain every slide is using the speech to support the visual aids instead of the other way around. If your slides cannot be simplified to meet the guidelines given earlier, consider using another medium, such as a printed handout.

Tables: A table is a special type of text file. A table is an arrangement of words and numbers in columns to illustrate relationships. A simple example is a table of contents, which identifies the page number for each subject by listing the subjects in one column and the page numbers in another. Most tables in printed material are too complex to make effective slides. If it is to be effective, a table slide must adhere to the same rules as other text slides (six lines of six words each). You may be able to pull selected lines from a large table to make your point. If this is not possible, and your speech depends on the table, you have little choice but to print the table and hand it out. In this particular situation, a speaker would be justified in projecting an unreadable copy of the table in order to point out on the screen the location of information, making it easier to locate on the printed copies.

Line Charts: Most of us were introduced to line charts in grade school when we had to draw them on graph paper. A typical line chart will have a vertical axis along the left margin and a horizontal axis along the bottom margin with a wavy or jagged line in the space defined by the axes.

If it can be kept simple, a line chart makes a very effective visual aid. You should use a line chart when you need to:

1. Show trends or movement in continuous data, such as trends in productivity. (Is productivity increasing, decreasing, or stable?)

2. Compare several sets of continuous data (changes in inflation compared to changes in the federal deficit over the last decade).

3. Predict future trends.

The line chart is designed to show trends or movement and is not a good choice when you are making a static comparison. If you wanted to show the relative market shares of three companies in the third quarter, a line chart would be a poor choice.

Many line charts in published books are impossibly complex. Some of these will have six lines or more weaving up and down. One line will be solid; another will be composed of dots, a third of dashes; the rest will have various patterns of dots and dashes. What we are really seeing is multiple charts superimposed. While book publishers may feel driven to this extremity by economics, you should not follow their lead. To keep your audience from getting confused, limit each line chart slide to two wavy lines (or three if you can keep the lines clearly distinct).

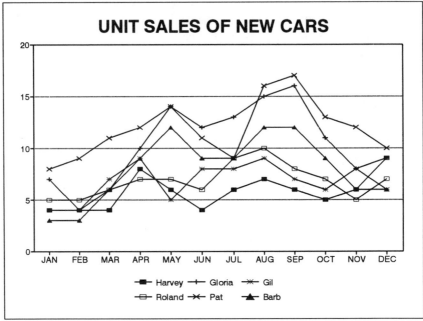

Figure 7-5 - Crowded line chart.

I have seen many presenters attempt to talk from line charts which are illegible from the back of the room. To avoid this misfortune, you should:

Simplify the scale on each axis.

Make every line bold.

Make every letter and number large and bold.

Column Charts: A column chart resembles a line chart in having both a vertical and a horizontal axis. In place of the wavy line, it has a series of vertical columns. A column chart also displays similar material. Typically, you would use a column chart to compare changes in size or magnitude over time. You can group up to three items to compare their changes over time. For instance, you might compare the percentage of new business failures in Japan and the U.S. over the last five years. At each year mark, you could have a red column for Japan and a blue column for the U.S.

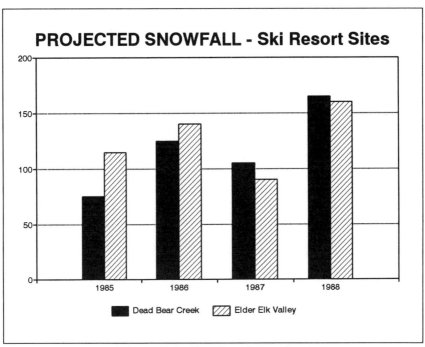

Figure 7-6 - Sample column chart.

Although their subject matter is similar, a column chart is by nature bolder and simpler than a line chart. If you have few points on the horizontal scale, you should choose the column chart. With many points, you should choose the line chart.

The Bar Chart: Whereas a column chart has vertical columns, a bar chart has horizontal bars. At first glance, a bar chart looks like a column chart turned on its side. But the two charts have another important difference: a bar chart has only one scale, the horizontal scale. The vertical dimension is only used for labeling the bars with the items being displayed.

With only one scale, the bar chart cannot show change over time. Therefore, it is typically used to make static comparisons, to show differences in magnitude between several items at one particular time. For instance, a bar chart might show the relative sizes of the armies of the U.S., the Soviet Union, China, and Iran in 1987.

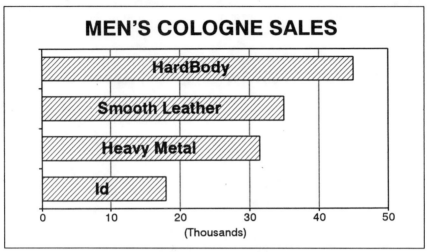

Figure 7-7 - Sample bar chart.

Because of its inherent simplicity, the bar chart usually makes an excellent visual aid.

Pie Chart: The pie chart also consists of a single scale, but the scale is configured as a circle. In its most common form, the circle scale represents percentages.

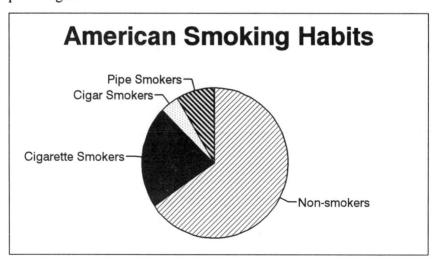

Figure 7-8 - Sample pie chart.

The only practical use of a pie chart is to show the relationship of component parts to the whole. It should not be used to compare component parts of more than one whole.

Arrange the pieces of a pie chart by size. Start with the largest slice of the pie; put the next largest next to it; then the third largest, and so on.

A pie chart becomes difficult to project clearly if it has more than five pieces in the pie.

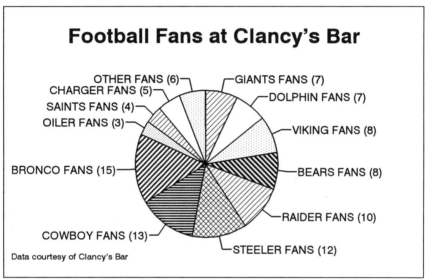

Figure 7-9 - Crowded pie chart.

Producing the Finished Product

Editing Slide Drafts: When you were working on your speech outline, you also designed your slides by scribbling drafts on pieces of paper. Now you must use each of those drafts as a guide while you produce the real thing. Before creating your actual slides, take a skeptical look at your drafts. You need to prune the stack, throwing out any which are unnecessary and simplifying those that remain.

Remember what Aristotle said – people are convinced if they hear sound logic from a trustworthy person while they are in a receptive frame of mind. Each of those requirements can be met only by a speaker who relates well to his audience. If your presentation becomes cluttered with too many fancy slides, you will lose that critical rapport with the audience.

In speaking, as in romance, nothing works like the human touch. People relate to people – not to images on the screen.

Using Outside Help: Once you have weeded out the unneeded drafts, you are ready to produce the final slides. Of course, if you are lucky, you can just send your drafts down to the graphics department. Or, if you have plenty of time and money, you can contract with a graphics or print shop to design and produce the slides. If you need sophisticated, multi-colored slides, but don't need very many, or don't need them very often, contracting with someone else to design and produce them is probably a good choice. Contracting the work saves you the expense and hassle of buying equipment and arranging training. Even if someone else does all the work, you should retain control over the designs. The operators in some graphics shops are not familiar with the design principles explained above. Those who are familiar will sometimes ignore the principles to produce whatever the customer seems to want.

On the other hand, if the slides you need are simple or you need to produce them frequently, you should consider doing the process in-house. Like everything else in the computer industry, graphics packages get cheaper and better every year. Consult your dealer on the best way to meet your needs, and, by all means, try before you buy.

Designing Inside/Producing Outside: Many graphics shops will let you save money by doing the design work yourself. By your providing the images on a computer disk, all they have to do is print them. To make this system work, you need a fairly modern PC. A Macintosh, IBM 386, or equivalent, equipped with a hard disk and any standard graphics program, should be adequate. You will also need to check to see which format the graphics shop prefers (PCX, TGA, IMG, etc.).

Visual Aids on a Shoestring: How fancy or expensive slides have to be depends on the nature of the presentation. Sophisticated graphics from an outside shop may be out of place at an informal briefing for a group of your peers. In that situation, you may want to rely on the simplest and cheapest of all production methods – hand-lettering with a transparency marker. Although an ordinary felt-tip pen looks similar, it will be much less effective on transparencies. Other situations call for clear, easy-to-read lettering, but nothing fancy. Should you find yourself needing to get the information across with no necessity to dazzle the audience, consider the processes described below. Each will produce acceptable slides, at low cost, with only a modest amount of work.

35mm Slides: One of the simplest ways to make high-quality text slides is to use movable letters and photograph them. Either borrow an existing system, such as the military uses for ID photos, or make your own. Graphic arts and business supply stores stock a number of letter sets which are designed to stick on paper and other surfaces. Other possibilities include the plastic letters included in many children's toys and the felt letters used to customize T-shirts. Possible backgrounds include whiteboards, table tops, and solid-colored carpets. It is a fairly easy matter to align the loose letters with a straightedge, then remove the straightedge and shoot.

If you have a computer hooked to a good dot-matrix printer or a laser printer, you can simply have your text printed extra large and photograph it. Printing the text on pastel paper will make the slides more interesting.

Charts present more of a challenge than simple text slides. If your computer has graphics capability, you can either photograph the printout or the screen. A photograph of the graphics on a color monitor can be stunning, but allow plenty of time for trial and error on exposure and lighting.

Without computer graphics, you can still produce acceptable charts, but it will take more time. You can create bar and column charts by carefully cutting and pasting construction paper. Line charts are possible using chart tape, a special narrow tape designed for use on wall charts. If you will be constructing a chart by hand, an overhead projector system is probably a better choice than 35mm.

Overhead Projector Slides: In the same time it takes to make a construction paper bar chart for 35mm you can make an overhead transparency chart – and you don't need to photograph it. Rather than construction paper, you would use colored acetate highlight sheets cut to size and stuck on a clear transparency. Most of the colored highlight sheets are self-adhesive, making the job easier. For a line chart, use transparent chart tape. Lining up the various bars and lines will be easier if you place the transparency over a sheet of graph paper.

Text slides present a different set of problems. In some situations hand-lettered slides will suffice. As mentioned above, use only transparency markers; ordinary felt-tip pens will not work. Put ruled paper under the transparency to keep the printing straight.

If your computer system includes a plotter, you can substitute transparency markers for the normal plotter pens and have the plotter draw your letters and lines directly on the transparency.

Judging from the overhead transparencies used in many presentations, many otherwise effective speakers seem to think anything which works on the printed page will work on the screen. Their transparencies are simply typed or printed pages run through a copy machine. Remember the six by six rules – no more than six words per line and six lines per page. If you pack many more than 36 words on the screen, the audience won't read them. A double-spaced typed page has around 250 words. I have even seen slides, which, on close examination, proved to have over 800 words per slide.

Fortunately, modern technology offers good alternatives to the type-and-copy syndrome. Several years ago, many people began making good quality, easily read overhead slides using a high quality dot-matrix or laser printer and a copy machine. The first step, of course, is to run off the text in a large font (24 points or higher). The rest is easy. Special 8" by 10" transparency film is available for both photographic copiers and thermal copiers. With the special film substituted for the usual paper, the copier will run normally.

Anyone using this process with a laser printer should be aware the process is now obsolete. Both 3M and Avery now make transparency products which will substitute for paper in a laser printer. Anyone with a laser printer can eliminate the copy machine step. The only problem you may encounter with this new process is a tendency for the transparency to jam as it is coming out of the printer. By exerting a slow, steady pull on the emerging transparency, you can prevent the jam.

If you don't have a laser or dot-matrix printer, but do have a copier which enlarges, you are still in luck. Simply print or type the text and enlarge it two or three times. On the last enlargement, make a transparency copy rather than a paper copy. The letters on the transparency need to be at least a quarter-inch high, but if you have room, enlarge them even more. While retaining adequate white space, you should make the letters as big and bold as possible.

WARNING! – A large office supply store is likely to have blank transparencies of ten different types for different applications. Although the transparencies look identical or similar, they are not interchangeable. Putting the wrong type of transparency in a copier or laser printer can damage the machine.

If all else fails, use stick-on letters on clear transparencies. The letters and the transparencies are available at office supply stores.

Framed or Unframed? Some speakers prefer overhead slides taped on cardboard or plastic frames; others prefer them unframed. Try both methods to see which you prefer. Some speakers who use framed transparencies, write all their notes on the frames and dispense with the index card outline. If you are going to use the same frames over, put your notes on 2" by 3" stick-on sheets (Post-it brand or something similar). Some people who intend to use frames over actually destroy quite a few by ripping off the old transparencies. You will find it much less destructive to slit the tape with a knife.

Frames also make it easier to use overlays (sequences of slides connected by tape hinges). Overlays are especially good for showing the development of a process. If you wish to reveal one bullet or sub-topic at a time, you can tape masks made of paper or light card stock onto the frame. Assume you need three masks on one slide frame. Cut the bottom mask to size, put it on the frame, and tape one side only. Then, size the middle mask, allowing substantial overlap with the bottom mask. Place the middle mask on the frame and tape down one side. Follow the same process for the top mask. When the masks are attached in this way, you can flip one after another, starting at the top, without worrying that one mask will get misaligned and snag on another mask.

The use of masks taped to slide frames allows you to work from notes while appearing not to. If you keep the notes short, you can print them in huge letters on the masks and dispense with tell-tale reading glasses. The note on each mask should suggest what to say *after the mask is flipped* because after you flip the mask, the note won't be readable. By glancing at the note just before you flip the mask, you will have the new topic fresh in your mind.

There is no such thing as a standard overhead frame. Dimensions vary greatly; try several sizes before you standardize. The larger sizes eliminate the need to mask the projector (more on masking later), but they will not fit in a normal file drawer. Dimensions for the hole in the middle of a frame also vary, but are usually fairly close to eight by ten inches. Be sure to leave an adequate margin on the transparency itself, so your text is not cut off. While you are standardizing, you should also settle on a single format. Either make all the slides vertical (portrait orientation) or all horizontal (landscape orientation).

For years, some speakers have been inserting their overhead transparencies in plastic page protectors. This system protects the slides and allows them to be stored in order in ordinary three-ring binders, but it does not allow any place for notes, and makes masks and overlays awkward. The 3M brand Flip-Frame™ transparancy protector is a variation on this concept. It is basically a page protector with a 1³/₄" by 11¹/₂" white flap on each side. When the Flip-Frame™ transparancy protectors are stored in a file or notebook binder, the flaps are folded inward, making the dimensions 9" by 11¹/₂". Before putting one of these on the projector, the speaker folds the flaps out. In the outward position, the flaps effectively mask the edges of the projector as well as the binder holes in the transparancy protector. Notes can be written on the flaps in pen or pencil. This system is harder to handle than conventional frames because two hands are required to open the flaps.

Many speakers prefer unframed transparencies because they take less time to prepare (no taping or inserting) and are less bulky. A Flip-Frame™ transparancy protector with transparency is four times the thickness of the transparency alone. Most people find unframed transparencies are harder to position on the projector. This problem can be simplified by buying or making a transparency holder. The easiest way to make a holder is to tape a conventional transparency frame to the bottom of the plastic box that new transparencies come in. If the plastic of the box is not clear, you can cut out the bottom and tape a transparency in its place. With the transparency holder taped to the projector, any slide tossed into the holder will settle into the right position. You can make it easier to remove each slide by taping a pencil eraser in one corner of the holder. Since the holder guides each slide into the same position, overlays work well, but the lack of individual frames leaves no place to write notes or attach permanent masks.

Because overhead slides are transparent, reading the top one in a stack can be difficult. The traditional solution to this problem is to interleave pieces of paper with the slides. Unfortunately, all the materials used for transparencies tend to hold static electricity, which makes the paper inter-leaves cling stubbornly to the transparencies. You can lessen this problem by using light card stock instead of paper; the cheapest light card stock is called Vellum or Vellum Bristol. I go one step further by dog-earing one corner of each vellum sheet, so I don't need to pry up the edge of a transparency with my fingernail.

Producing Flip Charts/Flip Cards

The lettering on flip charts and flip cards is rarely bold enough. Test each chart to see if the most distant audience member can read it.

You will find it easier to keep hand printing straight if you buy lined flip charts or pencil-in lines using a yardstick as a straightedge. For a more professional appearance, consider using stencils or a mechanical lettering system.

Felt-tip markers bleed through flip-chart paper. To prevent ruining the underneath sheet, stick a piece of cardboard under the top sheet. The cardboard back from a flip-chart pad is perfect.

If you want to remove one chart without revealing the next one, leave a blank page or two between them.

If you plan to draw something while you talk, pencil in guidelines to work from.

Testing the Finished Product

A slide that looks great as you hold it up to the light in your office can bomb when you project it during a speech because conditions during the speech are going to be very different. The light will be different. The audience will be farther away and some will see the screen at an angle. You should always rehearse with your visual aids. Before you start to rehearse, though, you should field test the slides under conditions which are as close as possible to the conditions under which you will speak.

While testing, project each slide and move to the far corners of the room. Ask yourself if every slide can be quickly grasped and if it has the effect you want. Be a hard-nosed editor: there is no such thing as a good slide which the audience can't read.

Executive Summary

1. While organizing the speech, you should sketch each slide you will need.

2. Text slides should have only one obvious main point, no more than six lines of text, and no more than six words to a line.

3. Print in both capitals and lower case letters.

4. Use plenty of blank space to make words stand out.

5. Make letters large and bold. On overhead slides, letters should be at least $1/4$" high.

6. Watch how TV advertisers apply these principles.

7. Column charts are preferable to line charts because they are bolder.

8. Beware of making graphics too complicated.

9. With the right supplies, you can make high-quality overhead slides directly using a laser printer.

10. Field test every slide.

8

Rehearsing and Visualizing the Speech

Giving a speech is like riding a bicycle: both require a coordination of physical and mental skills. You probably remember that from Chapter 1, but I have repeated it here to help you see what can go wrong in a speech rehearsal. Neglecting either physical or mental preparation can sabotage the speech.

Most problems in delivery can be traced to inadequate rehearsal time or inappropriate rehearsal conditions.

Solo Preparation

Both bike riding and speech-making require physical preparation. Trying to pedal a bike in busy traffic, when you have never pedaled one on a quiet street, can be terrifying, no matter how much mental preparation you have done. Likewise with speaking. Mental rehearsal is important, but it does not substitute for the physical act of giving the speech. Nothing you do in preparation for a speech is more important than delivering the speech at full volume enough times to feel comfortable with it. Even in the early rehearsals when you are alone and the speech is still very rough, saying it aloud is better than saying it to yourself, and saying it at full volume is better still.

The single most important ingredient in successful speaking is practice. The most effective type of practice is with maximum simulation. The way you give the actual speech will closely resemble the way you rehearsed it. If you rehearsed only in a soft voice in front of your mirror, you will probably deliver the speech either in a soft voice or in a loud voice which doesn't sound natural. If the words that flesh out your outline are ever to flow smoothly, your tongue needs to practice them as much as your mind does.

Timing

Saying the speech aloud also lets you time it accurately. For many people, silent rehearsals seem to run at a different speed without their being aware of it. By timing at the early rehearsal stage, you have time to add or delete material before memorizing the outline. To gain flexibility in timing, you should select a portion of the speech near the end which you can take out or leave in depending on how long the speech is running. After your rehearsals are running well, time the speech to the point where your optional material starts and write the time on your notes. Then you have a reference point to use in the actual speech when deciding to leave in or take out the material.

Rehearsing With an Audience

After a number of mental run-throughs to familiarize you with the outline, you should rehearse the speech just as you will give it. Use the actual room, if you can, or another of similar size; recruit friends or associates and a video camera to be your audience (station at least one person on the back row); hook up the projector and integrate your visual aids into the presentation; use full volume, full movement, and full gestures. Strange as it seems, the simple physical acts of talking loudly and moving forcefully will increase your confidence.

You may have difficulty arranging maximum simulation for all rehearsals, but you should attempt to have as many as possible under realistic conditions. Even if you must rehearse in a smaller room with no equipment, every action of your speech should be represented. For instance, if you are planning to use an overhead projector, but none is available for the rehearsal, hold up your slides (or a piece of paper) at the appropriate points in the speech. The audience may not be able to read the slides, but you will get experience in integrating the slide handling into your presentation.

After each rehearsal, poll your rehearsal audience:

Could each of them hear you clearly?

Were the visual aids easy to read from the farthest point?

Was the point of each visual aid obvious?

Did you handle the visual aids smoothly?

Was your overall organization clear?

Were any of your points unclear? Ask them to state your main point and major supporting points from memory.

Did you have any distracting mannerisms? (Jingling coins? Tugging at skirt? Playing with pointer? Pacing? Other?)

Was the pace too fast to follow easily?

Was the pace too slow to be interesting?

Did you maintain eye contact?

Did you run overtime?

After each rehearsal consider revising the presentation based on audience input. If the pace of your delivery was successful but you ran overtime, cut material rather than speeding up. Likewise, if the speech was too short, add material rather than slowing down. If you are to be persuasive, your pace needs to be right for the audience so they can absorb what you say easily without being distracted. If you tinker with the pace to cope with timing problems, the audience may miss key information.

Take care that multiple rehearsals do not result in a memorized speech. You should rehearse until every idea comes to mind easily and you can improvise an explanation of each idea without straining for words.

Focus on the Goal

Ed Oakley, a friend and colleague of mine, uses a marvelous analogy to explain coping with obstacles:

> *Imagine you are riding a bicycle down a path when you see a large rock ahead of you. If you focus on the rock, you will probably hit it. You must focus where you want the bike to go instead of where you don't want it to go.*

In the same way, when you are thinking about an upcoming speech, you should concentrate on the success you expect, not only for the speech as a whole, but also for its components. If you think about a joke, imagine the laughter which will follow. If you will use a shocking statistic, imagine the stunned silence which will follow.

Whenever you talk to yourself, say positive things. Instead of saying ''I hope I don't drop my slides again,'' say ''when moving slides, I will keep a secure grip and put them in an easy-to-reach spot.'' Always focus on the goal, not the obstacles.

Visualization

An elaborate version of the same principle is visualization. Bobby Darnell, now an oilman in Oklahoma City, played football for the University of Oklahoma during the period when Bud Wilkinson's teams won 47 games in a row. According to Bobby, when Bud Wilkinson would talk to the team after the last practice before a game, he would tell them to visualize the game before going to sleep. He wanted each player to think through his assignment on each offensive play, to see himself blocking against each of the opponents' formations. Since everyone played defense as well, every player also had to think through his defensive assignments, to see himself reacting against the various plays the other team might run.

Wilkinson believed if his players went through this mental exercise just before going to sleep, they would react instinctively during the game, while their opponents would have to think for an instant before reacting. That difference would give the Oklahoma players a one-step lead at every phase of a play.

In the same way, a tennis player working to develop her backhand will not only practice the backhand physically; she will also visualize the backhand mentally. In early practices, the physical backhand will be imperfect, but she can get the mental backhand exactly right. She must be able to convince herself that the perfect backhand is within reach, or she will never be able to do it physically.

Speeches follow the same pattern: an audience will not laugh at your jokes, relax and let their guard down, or accept your logic unless you believe they will. Creating that belief in yourself is the main purpose of visualization. The process of visualization involves no magic or mysticism; the simplest description I can think of is *directed daydreaming*. Visualizing turns your imagination loose, but with a definite goal in mind. The process I use and recommend has five steps:

1. Relax

2. Concentrate

3. Picture

4. Describe (optional)

5. Repeat

Let's take them in order. For the first step, relax via any method which works for you; some people take a warm bath; others listen to soothing music; I usually daydream about pleasant experiences. I relive floating in the warm sea off Pensacola or sitting beside a glacier-carved lake in the Rockies.

The second step – concentrate – means direct your mind to the speech. Either imagine the speech coming up or relive a past speech which was highly successful. Be very specific: imagine the exact room the speech will be in and your exact spot in that room.

The third step – picture – involves more than an inner eye. You should not only *see* what happens, but *hear* and *feel*, as well. Let yourself live the experience of the speech. Hear the moderator's introduction of you as inquisitive audience members turn to look at you. See yourself stride up to the platform. Feel your face fold into a smile and see audience members smiling back. Feel yourself move and hear your voice as you start talking. Watch the audience explode in laughter at your first joke; then hear them interrupt you with a *rebound laugh* as you start talking again. As you get into the logic of your speech, audience members smile and nod approvingly. You feel the hush descend on them in the emotional moments. As you finish, the audience bursts into thunderous applause. At that point you can come back to the here and now.

The fourth step – describe – is optional. The effect of visualization will be stronger if you describe it to another person, but you won't always be able to find a willing listener. When you describe it, talk in the first person and the present tense: "I hear the audience laughing and see them smiling," etc.

Finally, repeat the process, interspersed with rehearsals, until you believe the actual speech will happen as you have pictured it. After that it is simple: give the speech just as you practiced and visualized it.

Executive Summary

1. Rehearsing the physical aspects of a speech is as important as rehearsing the mental aspects.

2. Whenever possible, rehearse under conditions which are similar to the conditions of the speech.

3. When possible, rehearse with an audience and ask them pointed questions to see how you did.

4. Always focus on what you want to happen in the speech, not what you want to avoid.

5. Visualize yourself succeeding.

9

Relaxation Techniques

Unrelieved tension can reduce performance on any job, but during a presentation, the effects of tension are doubled. Not only does the speaker's tension affect the speaker, it affects the audience, as well. A typical audience, sensing tension in the air, can become markedly unreceptive.

General Relaxation

As we all know, a certain amount of stress is normal and desirable. In fact, normal people develop a rhythm, alternating between peaks of high stress and valleys of low stress. What we need to combat is the unrelenting stress that squeezes out our vitality and makes every task more difficult.

The speeches you give are not isolated from the rest of your life. If you have been stressed-out for three months, you can't expect a magic cure which will turn you into a relaxed person ten minutes before a speech. Therefore, you need a two-part strategy for coping with stress. You need to be a relaxed person generally and also learn some specific techniques for relaxing just before a speech.

Any public library will have a number of books with expert advice on teaching yourself how to relax. Most of the books agree that not everyone relaxes the same way. The suggestions that follow are some of the more popular tactics. Try them out and use the ones that work. If you have a suspense file (a.k.a. a reminder file or a tickler file) to keep track of your responsibilities, you may want to write down some of the ideas and file them so you will keep being reminded of the new habits you are assuming.

Develop friends. Good friends offer two good stress relievers: social support and objective insight. Social support may be nothing tangible, but knowing that someone else cares and understands has been proven to make stress more tolerable. The benefit of objective insight is more obvious. You may be so stressed-out you feel the world is caving in when you are actually facing only a minor setback. An objective friend can help you put things in perspective.

Identify the sources of stress. If you have a general up-tight feeling that seems to come from nowhere, look around for a source. People often suppress a stress-inducing problem (bad-tempered boss) because they can't deal with it in the way they wish (physical violence). The result can be a vague, general state of uneasiness and tension suffusing everything a person does. If you have that feeling and can identify the source, you can try to solve the problem (talk to the boss) or use some of these other remedies; perhaps talking it over with a friend. Sometimes, merely knowing the source is enough to relieve the tension.

Discuss the problem. Discussing it with a friend will help, but discussing it with the source is even better. Too often, we get angry over someone else's behavior (the boss, the spouse, the kids), but bottle up the feeling rather than explaining our side of the situation. A better approach would be to explain how we feel without getting angry or defensive. Sometimes the problem can be solved by discussion, but even if it isn't, stating our case is less stressful than holding in anger.

Take a walk. Walking does several things to reduce stress. It gives you a brief change of scenery, helping you detach from your immediate problems. It reduces muscular tension as you move several major muscle groups. And, unlike heavy exercise, it tires you slightly without increasing your adrenalin level (which would excite, rather than soothe you).

Have fun. Any recreation you enjoy, whether active or passive, will allow you to escape from yourself, to put your stress aside for awhile. The more you can lose yourself in the activity, the better, but beware of any competitive sport you feel you must win. A player who can't stand to lose will leave a game more stressed-out than before. If you are in that category, either learn to play for fun, or find another sport.

Exercise often. Even if exercise is not one of your favorite ways to spend time, you should try to exercise at least 20 minutes 3 times a week. The evidence is overwhelming that frequent moderate exercise will improve your health in general and reduce stress-related symptoms in particular.

Hug someone. Modern researchers have demonstrated what grand-mothers have known for centuries. Physical contact can be very comforting.

Reduce stimulants. The stereotypes of nervous coffee addicts and chain-smokers are generally true. If you can't cut out caffeine and tobacco, at least cut down.

Take an imaginary vacation. After you have been working steadily on something, give your mind a break. Lean back, close your eyes, and for two minutes imagine the sensory pleasures of the best vacation you know. If you like the beach, then feel what happens there. Feel the hot sand sticking to your feet. See the foam as the waves surge and ebb. Feel the wind whip your hair. Watch the sand crabs burrow into the wet sand. One of the secrets to relaxation is rhythm. You work hard at a task and then let it go for a few minutes of relief.

Take enough breaks. Tension gradually increases as you work. If you work long enough without a break, you will convince your body that being tense is its normal state. If you pace yourself by working hard and then taking a break, you will actually accomplish more over the long run.

Learn to say *no*. A major cause of stress is over-scheduling. To succeed, you will need a clear sense of your priorities. You don't want to get trapped always saying yes to your work and no to your family, for instance.

Delegate work. Too many managers believe, "If I don't do it, it won't be done right." Relying on others is a survival skill of the first order. Don't be afraid to ask for advice or help. If subordinates cannot handle a task, consider training them instead of doing it yourself.

Take a hot bath. My wife swears by this one. You don't even need to be dirty. Just fill the bathtub as high as you safely can, put a pad behind your head, then lean back and relax. Be careful not to scald yourself because extremely hot water adds to the body's stress.

Get a backrub. This is the old-fashioned massage – not the kind performed by the "discreet escorts" at the Blue Velvet (adults only) Lounge. Having your spouse rub the muscles, tendons, ligaments, and joints of your back, legs, and feet will induce partially contracted muscles to relax.

Try tensing and releasing. You can create an effect similar to a massage by yourself. Put on loose-fitting clothes (or loosen your belt and collar). Then, sitting in a comfortable chair or lying on the bed, alternately tense and relax one muscle group at a time. Start at your toes and work systematically. With each set of muscles, push hard to build up tension, then relax completely. Several repetitions will leave you as relaxed as a cat in a sunny window.

Look for sources of joy. Seek out the things you especially enjoy and make time for them at regular intervals. What you enjoy might be pick-up basketball or antique stores or painting ceramics. Whatever you enjoy most should have a protected spot in your schedule, no matter how busy you are.

Let tomorrow take care of itself. In a play I wrote some years ago, I had a Shoshone Indian patriarch utter this proverb: "Every road leads up the mountain and down the mountain, so do not ask where the road leads, but ask if you may walk it with a light heart." If that isn't an Indian proverb, it should be. Advance planning is a good thing; advance worrying causes heart attacks.

Breathe slowly. We all know that emotional states can trigger physical responses. (People under emotional stress breathe faster, for instance.) What is less well known is that by controlling the physical response we can sometimes alter the emotional state. By consciously slowing your breathing rate, you may be able to reduce your feeling of stress. Try to pace yourself by inhaling for four seconds and exhaling for five. After a couple of minutes, you should notice a change, both in your normal breathing and your state of mind.

Pray about it. Many people find talking to God can be liberating in the same way as talking to a friend, provided the communication channel isn't clogged with stilted, old-fashioned language. The most effective prayers for unburdening the soul are simple and direct, without posing and without ornamentation. Of all the things my wife has done for me, one of the most valuable is her oft-repeated advice to "give it to God."

Eat a balanced diet. Funny eating habits do funny things to body chemistry. Since speaking is a physical, as well as a mental, activity, you should pay attention to your physical needs.

Get plenty of rest. Of course, you should get plenty of rest before doing anything important, but it is especially desirable before an important speech, because lack of rest, in addition to making you tense, can cause you to lose your voice when you need it most.

Relaxing Before a Speech

Take a walk. If you have time to kill, take a stroll around the building. If you are in a meeting room, go outside and get a drink of water. This will ease your dry throat, as well as providing a chance to move around.

Have a mint. This is another good way to moisten a dry throat. Chewing gum is not so good; if you forget to spit it out, you can really gum up your speech. The tiny mints made by Certs and Tic-Tacs are small enough to be concealed in your mouth while you are speaking. Slip two or three of them between your lips and your teeth before you start. In that position, they will not interfere with articulation, and they will melt slowly, keeping your mouth moist for quite a long time.

Stretch and shake. If your shoulders are tense, step outside and stretch your arms over your head. Next, dangle your arms and shake them, letting your hands and fingers flop like a dishcloth.

Take a hard breath. Use your diaphragm to press your stomach out as you take a deep breath. With your diaphragm, press as hard as you can against your belt. Hold the breath and then blow it out through your mouth. Repeat this several times. You can actually do this one in the meeting room if you are fairly discreet.

Try isometrics. This is a less obtrusive version of the tensing and releasing exercise described in the previous section. Clasp your hands and press down with one while pulling up with the other, then release. Or, interweave your fingers and squeeze hard with both hands. Or, with your feet flat on the floor, imagine you are straddling the spindle of a turntable. Try to make the turntable turn by pushing down and forward with one foot while pushing down and backward with the other foot. Then reverse directions.

Wiggle your toes. One of the secrets to appearing calm when you badly want to fidget is to fidget in ways that can't be easily observed. Crossing your legs and swinging one of them is a bad choice, even if your legs are under the table. Wiggling your toes inside your shoes, on the other hand, is an excellent alternative because it is so hard to detect.

Imagine the audience naked. If you find the audience intimidating, look at them and imagine how they would appear in their birthday suits. Be careful with this one; depending on who is in the audience, it can get distracting.

Imagine the audience holding empty bowls. When Dottie Walters is offstage preparing to speak, she imagines herself holding an immense tray loaded with delicious food. She imagines each audience member holding an empty bowl, and as she comes out, she says to herself, "I have just what you need!"

Smile at the audience. If you smile at them, they will normally smile back. That eases things both ways. You appear more confident to them; they appear less intimidating to you.

Executive Summary

1. Being a relaxed speaker requires a two-part strategy. You must learn a relaxed lifestyle, and practice specific relaxation techniques just before a speech.

10

Keeping Track of What You Plan to Say

Speakers have available to them four basic methods for keeping track of what they will say:

1. They can write down every word and simply read the manuscript.

2. They can memorize every word.

3. They can work from a written outline.

4. They can work from a memorized outline.

The first two of these methods make it hard to be convincing. Reading every word usually makes the speech sound canned and makes eye contact next to impossible to maintain. On the other hand, in some situations, reading a speech is unavoidable. The President normally reads his speeches because the world is listening; one sentence poorly expressed can create an international incident. Managers are sometimes in a similar situation. What they have to say is so sensitive, they run it by the lawyers to check the wording. If you are ever in that situation, you should consider just handing out copies of a written statement. Most people find reading a speech to be very constricting.

Memorizing every word is not much better. You can maintain eye contact, but the speech is still likely to sound canned, and interaction with the audience is likely to throw you off. Trial lawyers, when faced with an opposing witness who is reciting a memorized account of an incident he did not see, may expose the witness in front of the jury by asking simple questions:

> LAWYER: *Would you tell us what you saw while you were behind the apartment building?*
>
> WITNESS: *Well, yeah, see, I saw this guy coming up the alley with a knife in his hand and then for some reason he goes up the fire escape.*
>
> LAWYER: *Let me ask you, was the alley dirt or gravel or asphalt?*
>
> WITNESS: *Well, I didn't pay no attention to the alley itself.*
>
> LAWYER: *Okay, go on from there.*
>
> WITNESS: *Well, yeah, see, I saw this guy coming up the alley with a knife in his hand and then for some reason he goes up the fire escape.*
>
> LAWYER: *Did you see or hear anyone else in the alley?*
>
> WITNESS: *What?*
>
> LAWYER: *Did you see or hear anyone else?*
>
> WITNESS: *Uh, no.*
>
> LAWYER: *O.K., so what happened next?*
>
> WITNESS: *Uh, well, I seen this guy coming up the alley with a knife in his hand and then for some reason . . .*

With enough repetitions even the dullest jury member will realize the witness can't pick up the story in the middle because he has memorized it word for word. He practiced reciting it from the beginning, so that is the only place he can begin.

The same thing can happen to a speaker who memorizes word for word. A couple of people interrupt with questions; then the speaker can't figure out how to get back into the speech.

For most people, the most practical alternative is using an outline, either written or memorized. The outline allows considerable flexibility in responding to the audience, while still ensuring all the important points get covered.

Outlining a Speech

As you probably have noticed, most experienced speakers who outline their speeches keep the outline on 3" by 5" index cards. Cards that size are small enough to be relatively inconspicuous. When they aren't needed, the cards fit easily into most pockets. For most speakers, the key-word outline works better than a sentence outline because the sentence outline takes too much space. For the same reason, only the most important ideas should go on the outline. If you forget a lesser idea and omit it, the effect on your speech will be virtually nil; the audience never knows what you don't say.

More than once, I have seen an insecure speaker bring up a deck of index cards three-quarters of an inch thick for a ten-minute speech. Typically, each card represents one minor detail. The speaker will say a sentence and flip a card, say another sentence and flip another card.

Ironically, success with this approach can set the stage for disaster. If the speaker is persuasive initially, the audience's thoughts begin to flow down the right channels. This encourages the speaker, who forgets the cards and talks heart-to-heart with the audience. Everything is as it should be – and then, disaster strikes. The speaker reaches a transition point and needs to check the next major point. He glances at the note card deck and realizes he has talked for five minutes without flipping a card. The card he needs, the one with the next major point, is buried 10 to 30 cards deep in the deck. He begins turning cards, carefully at first, then frantically. Eventually, he finds the right card and looks up to discover he has lost the audience.

Most people find it works better to have only one card, or at most three cards, with one to three words for each major concept. If, when you try this system, you find yourself constantly searching for words to express your ideas to the audience, the solution is not to put more words on the card. The solution is to rehearse more, so you become quicker at translating the outline into ordinary sentences.

Memorizing the Outline

As an alternative to note cards, you can memorize the outline, which is easier than most people think. One time-tested method for remembering a speech outline is the Places System. In fact, it has been used by speakers and other performers for 2300 years. The Roman orator Cicero (the same Cicero who "turned pale at the outset of a speech") was educated in Greece. While there, he picked up a legend about a poet named Simonides, who lived in the fourth century B.C. In that pre-literate age, poets could not live off book royalties. (Come to think of it, poets can't live off royalties in our post-literate age, either.)

Basically, poets in ancient Greece were performers. Today, someone with plenty of money who throws a party is likely to hire a band. Someone who threw a party in the fourth century B.C. was more likely to hire a poet. For a modest fee, the poet would recite one of his stock epics. For a more substantial fee, the poet would compose and recite a poem in honor of the occasion.

According to Cicero, a Greek nobleman named Scopas hired Simonides to provide entertainment for the guests at a banquet. Specifically, Simonides was to compose and recite a poem in honor of Scopas. On the night of the banquet, Simonides gave his best dramatic recitation, but when he concluded, Scopas announced that since the poem included lines in praise of the twin gods, Castor and Pollux, he (Scopas) would only pay half Simonides' fee. The other half could be collected from the gods Simonides admired so much.

Having already delivered his poem, Simonides had no recourse. (As a side note, this story illustrates why professional speakers try to collect their fees in advance.) Shortly afterward, a messenger came to tell Simonides two men were outside asking for him. Simonides went out, but saw no one. While he was peering around in the dark, the heavy roof of the banquet hall collapsed, killing everyone inside. The gods had paid their half of the poet's fee by saving his life. (This story sometimes comes to mind when I am studying my accounts receivable.) If you ever encounter an audience acquainted with this legend, you can make a great pun about a performer who "knocked 'em dead."

The story would end here except that the stone roof had crushed the bodies beyond recognition. When the next-of-kin arrived to claim the bodies, they couldn't tell which was which. But Simonides came to the rescue; he could name every corpse because he had memorized where every person in the banquet hall was seated.

Cicero commented that the feat was not too surprising since it was an extension of the method Simonides used to remember his poems. Simonides himself had said people wanting to improve their memories must "select places and form mental images of the things they want to remember and store those images in the places." You can use this same method. To make it work you need a sequence of "places," which are very familiar to you. You will then construct visual images linking your outline topics to those places.

To illustrate, let me explain the place list I use. I have constructed a list of spots or places in my house, arranged in the order I would logically pass them walking through the house. The first item on my place list is *hat tree*, because I see the hat tree immediately when entering through the front door. If I turn left at that point, I can go up a short flight of stairs to the L-shaped living/dining room. At that point, I can see directly in front of me an end table with a lamp on it, followed by a couch, followed by a matching end table and lamp. My second place is *lamp*.

The places need not be limited to furniture; a stain on the carpet or a crack in the wall would work just as well so long as you can visualize them clearly. I purposely avoided using the end table as a place because I planned to use the kitchen table and wanted to avoid any duplication. My third place is *couch*. Skipping the second end table and lamp, I come to some large foliage plants in the corner – my fourth place is *plant*. If I turn right at that point, I encounter a large overstuffed chair. My fifth place is *chair*. The list continues through 15 places, but 5 are enough to illustrate its use.

Actually, our living room no longer looks like this because my wife has rearranged the furniture, but for simplicity I have retained my original list.

With the places list firmly in mind, I can memorize a speech outline rather easily. Remember the mind map we made concerning productivity? Let's assume the first five points in a speech outline on improving productivity are:

1. Simplify Tasks

2. Write Simpler Operating Instructions

3. Hire Employees With More Skills

4. Improve Supervision

5. Increase Training For Workers and Supervisors

You recall the first five places on my Places List are:

1. Hat tree

2. Lamp

3. Couch

4. Plant

5. Chair

The 15 places on the Places List are in my permanent memory, so I can use them over and over as pegs on which I can hang any sequence of ideas I am working with. This system requires a substantial investment of time at the front end to construct and memorize the Places List, but after that task is done, you can memorize any other sequence quickly by hanging ideas on the permanent place pegs.

Here's how to do it:

1. Convert the first idea to a visual image or symbol.

2. Visualize the first place peg.

3. Visually connect the two images in your mind.

4. Convert the second idea to a visual image or symbol.

5. Visualize the second place peg. . .

The first major idea in the productivity speech is *Simplify Tasks*. The visual image representing that concept needs to be linked to the first place peg, which is *hat tree*. The easiest way I can think of to represent *Simplify* is to envision an old-fashioned circuit board, with its tangle of wires and tubes, and replace it with a tiny computer chip. If possible, the image should incorporate action, so I imagine the hat tree with old-fashioned messy circuit boards attached at various spots and an elf climbing up and down, yanking off the circuit boards and replacing them with computer chips.

HOW DID THE ELF GET INTO THIS? If having the slightly extraneous elf bothers you, the same concept could be symbolized by having each circuit board explode to reveal a computer chip beneath it. The important thing is to make the image unusual enough to be memorable. To aid in making the pictures distinct and out of the ordinary, I use the mnemonic APES:

A. Create an image with ACTION. (The elf pitches the circuit boards off the hat tree or the boards explode.)

P. See things out of PROPORTION. You could have a circuit board festooned with miniature hat trees. When the board explodes, it reveals a hat tree in the shape of a computer chip.

E. Use EXAGGERATION. You could imagine the hat tree being buried in hundreds of circuit boards, which are washed away in a flood and replaced with one computer chip.

S. SUBSTITUTE one item for another. Imagine a giant computer chip serving as a hat tree with hats hanging on its prongs.

You may be wondering if it wouldn't be easier to just memorize the words on the outline. For some people it would. Some people are more attuned to words than pictures, but for most of us the opposite is true. Most of us can connect quicker with pictures than with words. That's why computer systems which indicate commands with icons instead of words are considered more user-friendly. Most of us also dream in a *television mode* or occasionally a *silent movie mode,* rather than a *radio mode* (only hearing words without seeing anything). At some fundamental level our brains seem to prefer pictures.

Now that you understand how to construct one bizarre image linking a place peg with a concept, let's do the others.

1. Connect *Write Simpler Operating Instructions* with the place peg *lamp.* Imagine it is dark and the lamp bulb has burned out. You are holding a thousand-page operating instruction and, to keep the room from getting totally dark, you are burning one page after another in the empty bulb socket. You can afford to burn the thousand-page document because you plan to replace it with one page.

2. Connect *Hire Employees With More Skills* with *couch.* Imagine one employee sitting on the couch playing a tin whistle. From out of nowhere a one-man band appears complete with bass drum, snare drums, electronic keyboard, rhythm guitar, and harmonica. The one-man band takes control of the couch and boots off the whistle player.

3. Connect *Improve Supervision* with *plant.* Picture a slave master, complete with whip, glowering at the plants, which cower in fear. A fairy godmother sprinkles the slave master with magic dust which turns him into a genial orchestra conductor, who has the plants dancing in unison. You may notice it takes far longer to read this description than to visualize the image. Once you learn the system, it is very quick.

4. *Increase Training for Workers and Supervisors* connects with *chair.* Visualize a teacher behind a lectern standing on the chair and lecturing. Suddenly, another teacher vaults onto his shoulders, and another vaults on the top teacher's shoulders, and another on his, and another, *ad infinitum.* Naturally, they cut a hole in the roof, and the stack of teachers extends into the clouds.

Some people trying to use this system come up with rather ordinary images. For *Increase Training,* they might see a classroom with one student and many empty desks. That student would then be joined by four others. This realistic scenario lacks all of the qualities suggested by the APES mnemonic. Making the image realistic makes it less memorable. You can remember an outline using ordinary images, but it requires more effort. Memorizing a speech outline through a series of zany images connected to place pegs ensures the images will leap to mind whenever you try to recall them.

Having a recall process that is almost instantaneous gives you a certain freedom while you are giving the speech. Suppose you are giving this speech on productivity. You explain how tasks can be studied to find simpler methods and how operating instructions can be rewritten in a simpler form that is easy to use. You begin describing the plan for hiring workers with more skills, but someone interrupts with a question about simplifying tasks. As soon as you are through answering, another question comes up. You give full attention to the questions, as you should. Then, when you are ready to return to your prepared remarks, you must remember where you were. You start down the places pegs: hat tree – the circuit boards change to computer chips (did that). Lamp – burning the massive operating instruction (did that). Couch – the incredible one-man band kicks off the untalented whistle player (That's it – the plan for hiring workers with more skills.) You pick up where you left off.

If memorizing the outline seems a good idea to you, but you worry about the risk (What if I forget?), prepare note cards as a backup, but keep the cards in your pocket. If, at any point, you can't recall the next point, simply take the cards from your pocket, glance at them, and keep talking. Most of the audience won't even notice the shift.

Executive Summary

1. Reading a speech word for word makes it sound canned.

2. Memorizing a speech word for word makes it sound canned, and interruptions make the speech difficult to pick up in the middle.

3. The best method for retaining what you need to say is to memorize a key word outline.

4. If you will visualize and memorize a series of places you are familiar with, you can use those places as pegs to hang speech concepts on.

5. To connect a place to a speech concept, imagine a zany image combining the two.

6. If necessary, you can always carry note cards as a backup system.

11

Arranging the Room

Novice speakers often think arranging furniture and equipment in the room they will speak in is a simple matter to be done shortly before the speech. Actually, the process should begin with the earliest planning. When you are scouting the location (see pp. 33-34) to determine its feasibility, you should be thinking about possible arrangements, otherwise, you may paint yourself into a corner. For instance, you may plan your speech around 35mm slides and discover too late that the room cannot be darkened sufficiently. Or you may plan to spend half your allotted time in small group exercises, only to find the people and chairs packed so tightly they cannot break into small groups.

Advance Arrangements

After determining that the location is suitable, you need to communicate your desires as to how you want the room arranged. Your contact with the organization should be able to tell you who is handling the room arrangements. You should explain what you need over the phone and then reinforce your conversation by faxing or mailing a diagram: the more detailed, the better. At the same time you can list and explain your other requirements (What type of microphone? Any extra tables? What type of projector?). Be sure to take another copy of the diagram with you in case the original copy is lost.

Some rooms, such as boardrooms, gymnasiums, and movie theaters, allow little choice in set up, but most rooms are more flexible. In choosing the room arrangement, you are also choosing how you and the audience will interact.

Projector and Screen Placement: The number of experienced hotel staff, meeting planners, and speakers who do not understand where to place a projector and screen is astonishing. Consider the arrangement shown in Figure 11-1.

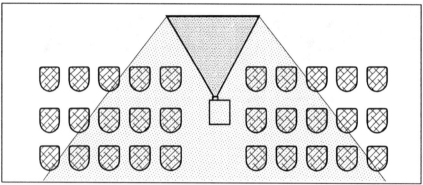

Figure 11-1

Placing the screen in the middle of the long wall guarantees people at the end of each row will not be able to see what is on the screen. In fact, the only people who will see it well are those in the shaded area. In addition, wherever the speaker stands on the platform, she will block the view of some people. The arrangement below (Figure 11-2) is better, but not optimal.

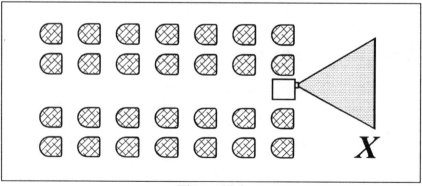

Figure 11-2

Placing the screen in the middle of the narrow wall gives more people a good viewing angle, but the speaker will still block the view of some people. The best place for the speaker is the spot marked *X* near the edge of the screen, but if an overhead projector is used, the speaker will need to return to it to change slides. If you plan to place a screen at the end of a rectangular room like this, you may need to bring in a larger screen. To ensure that everyone can read the screen, follow the *6X Rule: The distance from the screen to the farthest audience member should be no greater than six times the width of the projected image.* Figure 11-3 shows the best arrangement for this room.

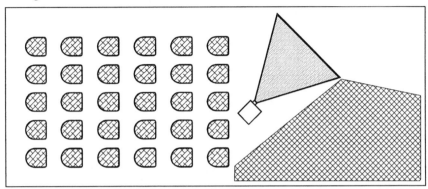

Figure 11-3

With the screen in the corner, everyone in the audience has a good viewing angle, and the speaker can move anywhere in the cross-hatched area without blocking anyone's view of the screen.

Sample Room Diagrams

Other situations will require other room arrangements. Which is the right choice depends on the room dimensions, the available furniture and equipment, and – most of all – on what you want to accomplish.

Horseshoe or U-Shape: As shown in Figure 11-4, this arrangement encourages discussion among participants. You should consider it any time the audience numbers less than 30.

Center Table: In some small rooms, this (Figure 11-5) will be the only arrangement possible. It is actually a variation on the U-Shape. Don't try it with more than twelve people. Some hotels refer to this arrangement as "Conference Style."

Office Meeting: This one (Figure 11-6) is your best bet for a small group if you cannot get a room with a conference table. You can stand behind the desk or walk in front of it. If you find yourself giving many

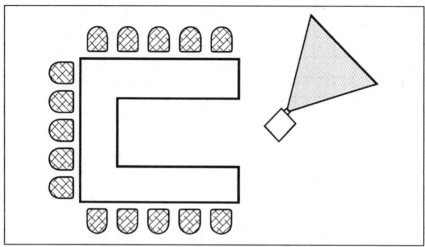

Figure 11-4 - Horseshoe or U-Shape room arrangement.

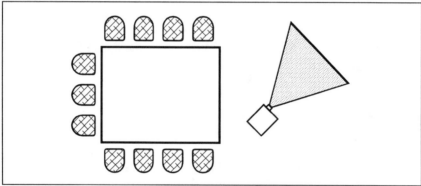

Figure 11-5 - Center Table room arrangement.

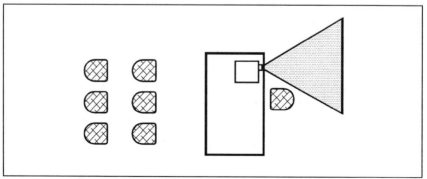

Figure 11-6 - Office Meeting room arrangement.

presentations with this setup, you should consider cutting out the projector and working from professionally prepared flip charts or flip cards.

Classroom: This is an effective arrangement (Figure 11-7) when you have too many people for the U-Shape. When a hotel tells you the capacity of a room, you should always ask if the number represents classroom style (with tables) or theatre style (without tables). Audience members always appreciate tables, which simplify note-taking and provide space for water glasses, coffee cups, and handouts. The *chevron* or *herringbone* pattern allows a wider center aisle and lets the participants see one another.

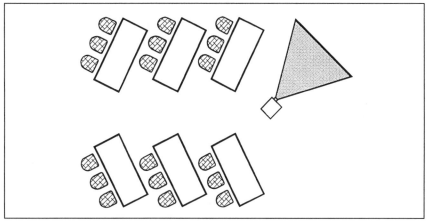

Figure 11-7 - Classroom arrangement.

Theater or Auditorium Style: This arrangement (Figure 11-8) is not ideal, but often necessary for large groups. Use the 6X Rule to ensure the screen is large enough.

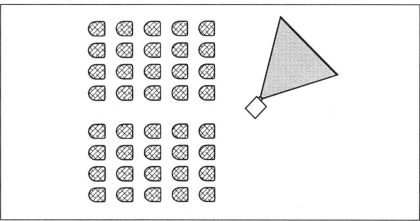

Figure 11-8 - Theater or Auditorium Style arrangement.

Amphitheater: In a well-designed amphitheater, each row is elevated above the row in front, providing excellent sight lines. This arrangement, as shown in Figure 11-9, maximizes the number of people who can be comfortably seated in a given space, though workspace for the audience members is severely limited. Because the seats are normally fixed in place, breaking the audience into small groups for an exercise can be very difficult.

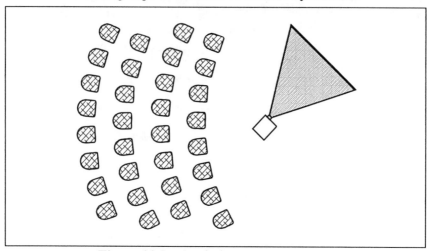

Figure 11-9 - Amphitheater arrangement.

Keystoning

To improve sight lines for the audience, projectors are often placed lower than the screen. This solves the problem of the projector blocking the screen, but creates another problem. When the projector is not on the same level as the center of the screen, distortion results. If the projector is lower than the screen, the distortion is called *keystoning* because the projected image is wider at the top than the bottom, like the keystone at the top of an arch.

Minor keystoning is usually ignored by the audience. If it isn't minor, you need to take corrective action. Raising the projector will bring back the original problem; a better solution is to tilt the screen. Some portable screens are equipped with an arm at the top, which has notches for the wire handle at the top of the screen. Place the projector where you need it and experiment with the notches until you have the optimal tilt angle.

A permanent screen requires a different solution. Some permanent screens are attached to the ceiling, others to a wall. To tilt a ceiling-mounted screen, pull the bottom of the screen back and tie it in place. Unfortunately, a wall-mounted screen lacks the clearance to pull the bottom back more than an inch or two. You can, of course, bring in a portable screen or move to more suitable facilities. Keystoning can also be corrected by altering the projector or the slides, but those solutions are more trouble than they are worth unless you give all your presentations in a room with a permanent keystoning problem.

On-site Inspection

It is a good plan to show up early for your speech and check to make sure everything is right. Once, when I was scheduled to talk at a convention, I checked the night before to ensure the room was set up exactly as I wanted. When I came down the next morning, it was totally different (unworkable). Moral: Take nothing for granted.

One contract I had with a public seminar company called for me to arrive in the lecture hall at least an hour-and-a-half before the scheduled starting time and to remain there until the seminar started. The reasons for the policy were sound, but when the speech or seminar starts early in the morning, it can be difficult to persuade whoever opens the room to show up more than an hour in advance. I advise every speaker to plan on arriving at least an hour early. With less time than that, you will be hard-pressed to correct anything you find wrong.

If everything is right, what does a speaker do with that hour? With everything in place, you can spend the time chatting with audience members. Remember, persuasion depends on trust. A few minutes in casual conversation can be quite helpful in building the necessary rapport with your audience.

What to Check

Even with the most diligent of room arrangers, the actual setup will only approximate the diagram. After checking out the audiovisual equipment, take a look at other possible problems.

Where will the audience sit? Are there any seats where the audience can't see the speaker or the screen easily. Chairs in bad locations should be removed or roped off.

Where will you sit? Sometimes the crew setting up forgets to provide a chair for the speaker, or picks a strange location.

Where will you speak? Check the route from your seat to the lectern. Are there cords to trip on? Loose steps beside the platform? Chairs, tables, or equipment in the way? Cracks in which you might catch a high heel? Either remove the obstacles or remember to avoid them.

Are there other distractions? Look around for sources of excessive noise or other activities which will attract the audience's attention. Some motel meeting rooms have a large plate glass window facing the pool. It takes a powerful presenter to compete successfully against well-shaped, suntanned bodies. Either close the curtains or face the chairs away from the window.

Can everything be left in place? If you will share the platform with other speakers, they may want different equipment, or the same equipment in different places. This situation is awkward, at best. A good approach is to set up your equipment exactly where you want it, then mark the spot with masking tape. Recruit someone else to make the equipment change so you won't be preoccupied during your introduction.

Executive Summary

1. Scouting the room in which you will speak is important to determine its suitability.

2. As early as possible, mail or fax a diagram of your proposed room arrangement to the person in charge of setting up the room.

3. The best location for a screen is usually in a corner.

4. To provide enough time to correct problems, a speaker should check the room arrangements at least an hour before the speech.

12

Delivery Techniques

Most speakers realize that good delivery is a key to success. The reasons why this should be so are not hard to find. As explained in Chapter 2, every speech is an effort at persuasion. Even an informative speech is an effort at persuading the audience to believe the information presented. As Aristotle noted, if the speaker is to succeed at persuasion, the audience must believe in the speaker's argument, believe in the speaker's character, and be in the right frame of mind. Each of these elements of success depends upon a strong delivery. The most powerful, most incisive arguments have little effect if the speaker's delivery is weak.

Delivery is often discussed as if it were a mechanical process or a formula. Supposedly, if you stand straight, talk loudly and clearly, maintain eye contact, and don't tug at your skirt or jingle the coins in your pocket, the audience will be swept off its feet.

Fortunately, delivery is *not* a mechanical process. It's more like courting your sweetheart. Doing and saying all the right things will not help unless you somehow touch the audience. To win the audience, you need to relate directly to them as a person who is warm, friendly, relaxed, and confident. All of which is hard to do if you are scared to death!

The first step, therefore, in the art of speech delivery is coping with speech anxiety. Every speaker feels nervous excitement before a speech; the good speakers have learned to channel that nervous energy to make the speech more dynamic. Consider the last time you saw someone in conversation who was really excited about telling a funny story or a family anecdote. You heard excitement in their voice, saw a face full of expression, and saw positive, forceful gestures. That storyteller was using nervous excitement as fuel for a dynamic presentation. He or she could have told the same story in exactly the same way on a stage in front of a microphone and captivated the audience, just as you were captivated. In your speeches, you should be able to harness nervous energy in the same way. Before reading the techniques described below, you may want to look back at the suggestions in Chapter 1 on facing fear.

General Guidelines

All of the delivery guidelines which follow are designed to help you relate positively to the audience, channel nervous energy into useful actions, and avoid distracting the audience.

Appearance: Your appearance should always be professional and appropriate to the occasion. Shortly before a speech, you should check your appearance in a mirror, or have someone else check it. Something as simple as a crooked tie or a slip that shows, something that would go unnoticed in your normal workplace, becomes glaringly obvious when you are in the spotlight. In one of my presentation workshops, one student gave a short speech (less than ten minutes) with his fly unzipped. I noticed because I was critiquing his appearance, but I was not sure anyone else noticed. On the next break he told me how embarrassed he was. I told him the audience may not have noticed. "Believe me, they noticed. Each one had to come up and tell me." Conversely, knowing you have a good appearance adds to your own confidence. Remember that a pleasant, relaxed smile improves any appearance.

Beginning the Speech: When the time comes, walk confidently to the lectern; look to make sure your notes, slides, and projector are in place; make eye contact with the audience; pause; smile; and begin. No one expects you to begin instantly. By pausing, you can collect the attention of the audience members, establish your initial contact with them, and orient yourself.

Language: You will normally be working from an outline, either memorized or on a card, as explained in Chapter 10. Working from an outline will help you keep the order of your ideas straight as you improvise the words to explain them. You should avoid clichés, but otherwise choose the phrases you would use in informal conversation. Many years ago, the Air Force forced 39 other officers and me to sit through a twenty-minute lecture by a dentist. He stressed the importance of "proper oral hygiene" with particular attention to "maintenance of dental interstices" and the "dental-gum interface." Not once in twenty minutes did he say, "brush your teeth to prevent cavities and gum disease," even though that is what he meant. To get your ideas across, you must present them in common, everyday language. Avoid choosing stilted, formal words which obscure your meaning and limit your ability to bond with the audience.

Be careful not to go to the other extreme and descend to the sort of coarse vulgar language which offends many people. Last year I heard a speech by a world-famous psychologist, a man whose insights over the last 35 years redefined our concepts of how emotions are generated in people. I also knew he was treated like an outcast by many other psychologists for reasons which were inexplicable to a biographer. I paid a sizable admission fee and joined several thousand other people in a standing-room only crowd.

He spoke mainly on relations between men and women, including sexual relations, using mostly locker-room words with some random (and graphic) clinical terms tossed in. After an hour of this, we received a twenty-minute break to allow us to purchase some of his books from the display in the lobby. While I was thumbing through a book, someone called my name. I turned and saw a woman who had taken one of my speech workshops two years before. She immediately asked how I felt about the speaker's language. Before answering, I asked how she felt.

"The reason I asked," she said, "was because in one of my speeches I said *bastard* and you said my choice of language might turn off part of the audience. What he is doing is a lot worse than what I did."

I told her his word choice didn't bother me personally, but I thought it might offend a number of people in the audience. I had puzzled over why he was using X-rated language, but I couldn't think of any valid reason. I had tried to read the audience's reactions, but they seemed to be hiding their emotions. Whatever he was trying to do, I said it was definitely a high-risk strategy.

When we returned to the lecture hall, one-third of the chairs were empty. One-third of the paying customers had left. I leave you to draw your own conclusions.

For reasons that are not altogether clear, some people who curse and tell dirty jokes in private, feel offended hearing the same words and jokes in public. In the early 1970's, I was acquainted with a gifted storyteller whose repertoire included very descriptive accounts of his sexual exploits on a university campus before World War II. After my wife and I saw *That*

Championship Season at the local university theater, I suggested he might want to take his wife.

That Championship Season is largely forgotten now, but it enjoyed a profitable run on Broadway and gained temporary notoriety for being the first stage play to break the taboo against the most notorious four-letter word in the language. To the best of my recollection, the word was spoken from the stage twice in this college production. The off-color storyteller was so offended he vowed never to attend another play at the college.

When you are considering whether to use a particular word or story, consult with people who know the audience, and carefully calculate the probable gains and possible risks. Then remember, speaking is like playing the horses: in the long run, you can't make money by betting on every long-shot.

Posture and Movement: The way you stand and move cues the audience as to your interest in them. A relaxed, confident bearing and easy, natural movement aids in establishing the rapport which is essential to success. When standing still, you should stand erect without being stiff. Keep half your weight on each foot rather than shifting back and forth, which is distracting to the audience. If you find it difficult to keep your weight on both feet, try standing with your feet farther apart. For good balance, the distance between your feet should be about the width of your shoulders. If you still keep shifting your weight, you may need to change to more comfortable shoes.

Use purposeful movement rather than random pacing. Deliver part of your speech from one spot, then move on the transition and deliver the next point from your new location. Only the most formal presentations require you to remain behind the lectern. An audience will feel closer to you if there are no barriers between them and you. Consider stepping toward the audience to emphasize important points.

Working only in the front of the room, as most speakers do, limits your contact with people in the back. For that reason, I use the whole room as much as possible. In a one-day seminar, I will go into the side aisles quite often. From a position on the side, I can still face everyone in the audience, and I can get much closer to people in the back corners. Audience members have to twist around in their seats to see me, but, provided they don't do it too long, changing position is worthwhile in itself. I also work the center aisle, but I only go into the audience about a third of the way, and I don't stay there long because people in the front rows can only see my back. Once in a while, I will even talk briefly from the back of the room.

So far as possible, I try to increase contact with people in the back of the audience by spending more time with them when working the crowd before a speech and during the breaks. For the same reason, when the audience is doing an exercise, I usually observe from somewhere in the back half of the room. Since I am not talking, I can use the back half of the center aisle.

Gestures: An audience wants to relate to a live human being, not a robot. Too often, speakers let their natural anxiety impede their natural gestures. To keep from being motionless, they program specific gestures at specific points in the speech. The result is predictable, sort of like the steel and rubber Abraham Lincoln at Disneyland. Other speakers attempt to solve the problem by ensuring their hands don't move. They either clutch the sides of the lectern, clutch both hands together, or keep their arms crossed.

The solution is elegantly simple: stop forcing things and let your hands make whatever gestures seem natural. When I explain this principle to someone for the first time, the most common reaction is ''but I talk with my hands.'' The fact is, most people who get thoroughly involved in telling something talk with their hands. Watch anyone, who is really animated, talking to friends and every point will be accentuated with a hand movement. Gestures only become annoying if they are extremely repetitive or unrelated to what you are saying (i.e., fidgeting). In speaking, as in conversation, the most appropriate gestures are likely to be unconscious. You should gesture in a speech exactly as you gesture when telling your favorite story to a friend. Some speakers modify their automatic gestures by making them broader, so they will carry to the last row of the audience, but other successful speakers make no apparent changes. You can make it work either way. At points in the speech where you don't feel like gesturing, let your hands drop to your sides.

Eye Contact: Every adult knows speakers need eye contact, but not everyone knows why. The purposes of eye contact are varied: it keeps the interest of the audience, since it is hard to ignore anyone who is looking at you; it reinforces the audience's perception that you are a trustworthy person; and it allows you to keep track of the audience's reactions. That feedback from the audience can be critical in the art of persuasion. If you are explaining a point in a presentation and you see the primary decision-maker frown, you should immediately comment or ask an open-ended question to draw out the person's objection. Sentences that consistently work well include:

Apparently, you have some reservations on this point.

What questions do you have at this point?

Hidden objections are very hard to answer. By getting the objections out on the table, you will be able to deal with them.

To keep the audience engaged by eye contact, you should not let your eyes dart about or steadily sweep the room. Look at one person long enough to make one point or one sentence, then look at another person. Try to look at people in different areas of the room so you draw in all sectors of the audience. In a large audience, people will not know for sure whether you are looking at them or someone close by. By singling out individuals in all areas, you can leave the impression you are talking directly to everyone.

Male speakers, especially, need to be cautioned about staring off in space. In our society, a man conversing about a serious, personal topic will glance at the listener from time to time, but will spend more time staring at the floor or the ceiling or out the window. The more important the topic, the more time the man spends looking away. However, when listening, the man will spend more time watching the talker. On the other hand, women, when talking seriously, are much more likely to observe the other person. You can verify these observations yourself simply by watching people converse about serious topics.

When giving speeches, most people carry over the habits they have in conversation. What this implies for most men is the need to change a deeply ingrained habit when learning to speak to an audience. Complicating the situation is the fact that most men (as well as some women) think their eye contact is better than it is. To find out how you are doing, ask the people in your rehearsal audience and your real audience. Depending on your habits, videotaping can be helpful here. A video camera will clearly show when a speaker is staring at his feet, though it may not show when he is looking out a window instead of at the audience.

Pace: The pace of a speech should never be thought of in terms of words per minute. The reason for this can be shown by a simple analogy. Imagine yourself holding a bucket of tennis balls and throwing them, one at a time, to someone across the room. Each ball he catches, he puts in a basket. You have two ways of making him miss. You can throw them in rapid succession, so the next ball arrives before he has disposed of the last one; or you can throw the first ball and hold the second until you see him distracted, then throw it when he isn't looking.

Now, imagine the ideas in a speech are those tennis balls. If the pace is too fast, ideas will be flying faster than the audience can grasp them. If the pace is too slow, the audience will start ruminating about tomorrow's tasks or tonight's date and miss major parts of your speech.

Establishing the correct pace depends on feedback from eye contact. You should present one idea and as soon as you see people have grasped it, present another.

When pace is thought of in this way, it becomes obvious that the pace is likely to be different in different speech situations. The concepts in my workshop on Dealing With Difficult People are easy to understand, though hard to apply. Because the concepts are easy to grasp, I talk at a very fast pace to hold the audience's attention. I also teach Survival Grammar, the grammar people need to survive in a modern office. For most people, grammar was one of the toughest subjects in school, and it is even harder for adults after a long layoff. In that class, I say a sentence and then wait as people wrestle with the concept. When I see nods or the glint of recognition in the audience's eyes, I state the next concept.

When you give the same speech more than once and optimize the pace each time, the length will vary. With some speeches, that's no problem, but in other situations, you have time constraints to deal with. Avoid the temptation to fix the time problem by adjusting the pace. If you find your speech running long because the best pace for a given audience is slower than expected, *don't speed up*! Since you already have the best pace, speeding up will cause the audience to lose some of your information. A better solution is to drop less important material. As explained earlier, you can build in flexibility by having some optional material just before your final summary. Whenever you are running short and leave it in, it fits. When you are running long and take it out, nobody guesses anything is missing.

Voice. For simplicity, we can think of the speaking voice as having four characteristics: volume, articulation, pitch, and rate. Volume and articulation are critical if the audience is to understand you. Fortunately, they are also somewhat interchangeable. If you have a sore throat and must speak softly, try to compensate by making your enunciations very distinct. Conversely, when you are speaking to an audience unfamiliar with your accent and style, speaking a little louder will make it easier for them. (This is the same principle as turning up the radio when a station is coming in garbled or broken.)

Whenever you anticipate a listening barrier based on dialect, accent, or vocal style, in addition to speaking loudly and clearly, you can adjust the organization of the speech. If the listening barrier is surmountable, the audience members will gradually improve in their ability to interpret what they are hearing. For that reason, when I work in the UK or in Australia and New Zealand, I start with material that is interesting but not critical (including funny stories). That gives the audience a little time to adjust to my accent before the important information hits them.

In any speaking situation, with or without the accent/dialect problem, you need to speak loud enough for the farthest audience member to hear clearly. Deciding how much volume is appropriate is not as difficult as it sounds. Experienced speakers can usually judge the appropriate volume just by looking at a room. A surefire way is to test the room. Have a friend stand in the empty room as far away as the farthest audience member will be. Then practice your speech with feedback from the friend. Remember, you will need to add a little volume with an audience because sound does not carry as well in a room full of people as it does in an empty room. You can also station a friend in back during the actual speech to give hand signals about your volume.

You should articulate clearly, but not overdo it. Only Paul Harvey and Howard Cosell can get away with that.

Your rehearsal audience can also coach you on pitch and rate. If you are speaking too slowly or your voice is too low key, harness your nervous energy to pump more excitement into your voice. If your voice is normally okay, but it shifts into a monotone when you speak, anxiety may be causing your chest and throat to tighten. Tilt your head forward (relaxing your throat muscles) and take several deep breaths using your diaphragm. Tilting your head forward will also help lower the pitch of your voice if it is too high.

If excitement makes your rate of speech too fast, try consciously stopping after every sentence or phrase. Far from detracting from your speech, these planned pauses can help persuade the audience you are careful and deliberate. If your rate of speech is too slow because you are frequently struggling to think of the next word or phrase, more rehearsals are in order.

Some people seem to have more voice trouble than usual when they speak early in the morning. If you suffer from allergies, post-nasal drainage, or a stuffy head in the morning, get up early enough to let your symptoms subside before the speech. Whether you suffer from these complaints or not, you need to be sure your voice is warmed up before an early speech. The muscles that produce and control your voice need to be warmed up for the same reason your legs need to be warmed up before a sprint. Serious exertion before warming up can cause an injury.

When you speak in the afternoon, warming up is likely to take care of itself since you probably talk off and on all day. Even so, a warm-up wouldn't hurt. Anyone who has taken singing lessons and remembers the warm-up exercises can just do those. Singing itself can be a good warm-up if you start with songs that are slow and in the middle of your range. *America the Beautiful* and old-fashioned sentimental songs like *Edelweiss* and *Tell Me Why the Stars Do Shine* work best. A more mundane approach used by some radio announcers is to take a deep breath and say "ahhhhhh-hh" sustaining it as if you were singing. A variation is to alternate "ahhhhhhhh" in the upper half of your range and "uhhhhhhhh" in the lower half.

Professional speakers, and others whose cash flow depends on a working voice, learn to be alert to the first sign of throat trouble. As soon as you detect your throat is getting sore, do something about it. Modern medicine can knock out most throat maladies rapidly, but there are no shortcuts to getting your voice back once you have lost it.

Keeping your head and throat warm in the winter is good preventive medicine. If you see some guy wearing a hat and scarf while everyone else is bare-headed, he is either an actor, a speaker, or a certified eccentric.

One home remedy worth mentioning is hot water with honey and lemon juice. Generations of actors swear by it with good reason – it works. If you are getting hoarse but must keep speaking, this potion will pull you through when nothing else can. Put a heaping teaspoon of honey and a squirt of lemon juice in an ordinary coffee cup and add the hottest tap water you can find. Stir until the honey dissolves; then let it cool until you can sip it. This mixture coats the back of your throat, so speaking does not increase the damage. It even looks like weak tea, so you can sneak it into a reception, if necessary. I once started a month-long tour with a bad cold and sore throat. Since I had to speak almost six hours a day, I was worried, but by sipping three to six cups of this stuff each day, I got through it all with my voice intact.

Using a Microphone: Giving a speech without a microphone is always simpler than giving a speech with a microphone. All types of microphones can have trouble with feedback squeals, sound distortion, interference, and static. All microphones take precious minutes of preparation time to get them properly adjusted. All are subject to breakdown, and all require at least a small part of your attention while you are on stage.

As long as you can be clearly heard by everyone without a microphone, don't use one. The effort it takes to project a little louder will make your life noticeably simpler.

In those situations where you have no choice, a few guidelines will help you minimize the difficulties.

All common speaking microphones are stationary, hand-held, or lapel-mounted. A stationary mike is always hard-wired, which means it has an electric cable or cord attached. Each of the other types can be either hard-wired, or cordless, which means it uses a radio transmitter to send the signal to the amplifier. All types vary greatly in quality and price. In addition, many facilities where you might speak do not maintain their equipment very well and some of them do not even have technicians who understand the equipment. Rental outlets for audiovisual gear usually have high quality equipment and they try hard to maintain it, but the equipment gets heavy use. Consequently, unless you bring the equipment with you, you won't know what performance to expect. Some professional speakers do carry a microphone with them – usually a state-of-the-art cordless lapel type. A few even bring amplifiers. With your own equipment or someone else's, test everything and, if possible, have a backup system warmed up and ready to use.

In some situations you will have a choice of microphone types; in other cases you won't. Of all the types of microphones, the most restrictive, by far, is the stationary mike built into a lectern. If you must use a mike and this type is the only one available, try to swivel it to the side, so you can stand beside the lectern to talk.

The choice between hard-wired and cordless really boils down to which set of problems you want to risk. For equipment in the same price range, hard-wired models usually have slightly better sound quality, but they have that awkward cable, which has to be dragged everywhere. Although cordless types eliminate the cable, they can be surprisingly finicky. Some rooms have radio-mike dead spots where the system won't work. Since the units work on CB frequencies, some will broadcast truckers' conversations to the audience. Radio systems also make possible the monumental speaker error of wearing the transmitter to the washroom without turning it off. If you choose to work with cordless systems, make sure you have spare batteries.

Some professional speakers prefer hand-held microphones; others opt for lapel mikes. Hand-held models sometimes have better quality. (All the components can be larger.) They also can be used as props. They confer an aura of importance since audiences have seen so many singers and roving reporters use them. However, they tie up one hand; if you are manipulating very many other things, like overhead transparencies, a hand-held mike can become very frustrating. Lapel mikes (also called lavalieres) have a similar problem if they are hard-wired; any time you move, you have to use one hand to maneuver the cord. Some lapel mikes are also narrowly directional; if you turn your head away from the mike, it won't pick up your voice.

Whatever type mike you use, get someone to help you check it out. I am convinced the checkout method used by most technicians is backwards. They typically make preliminary adjustments, then hang the mike on the speaker or hand it to her and ask how it sounds. The problem is that the speaker needs to know how it sounds *to the audience*, but it is impossible to tell while talking into the mike. A better system is to recruit someone with a voice like yours (same sex anyway), give that person the mike, and wander the audience area yourself to check the effect. Try to get the system adjusted low enough that people won't notice the mike is on (no distortion), but everyone can still hear clearly.

Use of Names: One of the best ways to get an audience intimately involved with a speech is to mention individual audience members by name. You may have noticed that more skillful politicians reply to newsmen by name in press conferences. They do it for the same reasons you should. It is almost impossible to stay uninvolved if someone calls you by name. Even those members who are not named become more involved as they sense a give and take between the speaker and the audience. A skillful use of names can give the impression you are having a conversation instead of making a speech. Sometimes you can plan the use of names when you are organizing a speech:

As Martin and I were discussing this issue last week. . .

At other times, you can adapt to something said a few minutes earlier:

Maria, when you were describing projected revenues, you raised a question. . .

At still other times, the feedback you receive during a speech will prompt you to name an audience member:

Now, Neal, I can see you think we have gone too far, but if you will let me explain this next point, I think it will relieve most of your concerns.

To be effective, the use of audience names should seem natural, just as it does in conversation. Unless you are already in a confrontation, you should not call a name to put someone on the spot.

Timing: In almost every speaking situation in business and government, staying within time limits is important. Often it is critical. Unfortunately, staying fully engaged with the audience makes it hard to watch the clock. The good news is staying aware of the time is definitely a learned skill, so you can learn it too.

In your early assessment of the speaking situation, find out what the time limits are, even if they are approximate. Time every rehearsal, even the early ones, so you develop an innate sense of how long different versions of your material typically run. As suggested earlier in this chapter and in Chapter 4, build flexibility into your presentation by putting in optional material near the end. In later rehearsals, set the most effective pace for the presentation using audience feedback. (See *Pacing* above.) Once the pace is set, adjust your material so each run-through falls midway between the upper and lower time limits.

Some speakers who follow the guidelines in the paragraph above can consistently come within ten seconds of their target time with no additional help. For most of us, additional assistance is in order. A watch or stopwatch on the lectern can help, provided you can read it and you note the time when you start. If the room you are in has a clock where you can read it easily, you may need nothing else. Professional speaker Orvel Ray Wilson likes having a clock on the wall so much he takes a battery-operated clock with him. In any room without a clock, he tapes his on the wall. I do the same thing when I teach seminars, but I put the clock beside the overhead projector where I can see it but the audience can't. (I can't read my watch at that distance, but I can read a clock.) On breaks, I prop the clock up on the projector, so the audience can see it.

All of us can think of situations where time limits are critical. The reason may be something dramatic – the decision maker has to catch a flight to Tokyo – or something mundane – "All conference sessions must end ten minutes before the hour so participants can get to the next session." In those cases, you may want more assistance.

The last time I chaired a panel discussion at a national convention, each panelist delivered a short presentation before we opened the discussion to questions. We had a simple system to keep each panelist on schedule. After introducing each person, I would sit on the front row and start timing. When we were within four minutes of the end of the allotted time, I would hold four fingers in front of my chest; the speaker could see the gesture, but no one else could. We had similar signals for "three minutes left," and so on. I have worked in other forums where the numbers were printed on flash cards. You are likely to have attended meetings where this system was used without your being aware of it.

To keep the system unobtrusive, the timer needs to sit on the first row or stand in the back of the room. At the annual Speakers College, which the Colorado Speakers Association hosts for the business and professional people of Denver, we go a step further. The Speakers College is an all-day event with a series of presentations by professional speakers, who waive their usual fees of $800-$6,000. We tell each speaker we will have a timer on the front row with flash cards and ask if the speaker wants any cues. (Most do.) We also explain our time's up signal, which is not optional. If the speaker doesn't stop by the end of the allotted time, the sound operator begins a very slow fade-in of music on the loudspeakers. The speaker recognizes the music as a signal and goes into his or her finale; the audience just thinks it is part of the show.

Whatever variation of this system you use, make sure the speaker and timer are absolutely clear on what each cue means. Especially beware of any confusion over whether the numbers mean *time elapsed* or *time remaining*.

On the Day of the Speech

If you have organized a good speech and have rehearsed it well, you will handle the inevitable nervousness without a hitch. In time, you will learn to thrive on the pre-speech excitement, but several pieces of advice are still in order.

You should not eat a heavy meal before you speak. You need to be on your toes – lean and hungry, as they say. If you are speaking at a lunch or dinner meeting, the excitement will likely dampen your appetite, anyway.

As mentioned before, arrive early to check the arrangements. Is the equipment where you expected it? Has the extension cord that threatened to trip you been taped down? Is the route from your seat to the lectern clear of obstacles? If you are the first speaker at a meeting, you should put up your first slide and focus the projector.

Check the order of your slides.

If you don't know the meeting moderator, introduce yourself. This would be a good time to review arrangements, such as time limits, order of speakers, and the method for handling questions. If you will be introduced, give the moderator the introduction you prepared on yourself and ask if she has any questions. Point out anything in the introduction that is crucial to your remarks.

After checking the arrangements, relax and chat with the audience members. A smile and a little bit of small talk will go a long way toward establishing the bond you must have to persuade someone.

Handling Questions

For a detailed discussion of how to deal with questions, see Chapter 14. However, the general comments which follow cover most situations.

1. Take questions from different parts of the room.

2. Repeat each question. Use paraphrasing to focus the unfocused question and soften the hostile question.

3. Defer your answer until the break if a question concerns only one person or is off the subject.

4. Direct your answers to the entire audience.

5. Avoid belittling or condescending answers.

6. Be ready to cut off questions because of time.

Awkward Situations

If you give enough speeches, you will eventually be put in a situation where the fates seem to conspire against you. Consider these situations drawn from real life:

A literary society has asked you to talk about Tennyson's poem *Crossing the Bar*. You plan to say the poem's sentimentality has made it popular out of all proportion to its poetic merits, which are few. Just before the meeting starts, an elderly woman presses your hand warmly and tells you with tears in her eyes how thrilled she is to hear you talk about

Crossing the Bar. The poem meant so much to her when her dear husband died that she keeps it by her bedside and reads it often in memory of him.

A statewide organization of speakers clubs has selected you to receive their Speaker of the Year award. They have asked you to be the featured speaker at their annual banquet and to speak for 25 minutes. About three minutes before your speech is to begin, the state chairman leans over to tell you the program is running behind. She asks you to cut your speech from 25 minutes to five minutes.

When you face a situation which seems to require a radical last-minute alteration in your speech, step back for a minute and take stock of the situation. Try to gracefully sidestep the dilemma if you can. If you can't, then use your best judgment; with enough imagination, many difficult situations become workable. Whatever you do, remember to stay within your own capabilities. A slam dunk is the highest percentage shot in basketball – but not if you are 5' 6" and 40 years old.
Here are the solutions adopted by the real-life speakers described above.

The speaker at the literary club spoke briefly on the sentimentality of *Crossing the Bar* and then moved on to discuss other Tennyson poems. He was able to make this shift successfully because he had taught several classes on Tennyson and could remember a number of interesting points and examples which were not in the planned speech. The gambit worked because the widow thought sentimentality was a compliment, while the literary club members understood that sentimentality is not a trait normally associated with great poetry.

The Speaker of the Year had prepared a tightly-woven, carefully timed, spell-binding speech – in other words, a *tour de force* worthy of the award. A moment's reflection convinced the speaker he could not possibly cut the speech to five minutes: it would be unrecognizable. He told the chairman his speech could not be cut that drastically, but he had an alternative. He would let the chairman present the award to him and then improvise a two-minute speech thanking her for the award and praising the organization's accomplishments. Since the ball was now in her court, the chairman reluctantly accepted the original plan; the speaker delivered his original speech and received a standing ovation.

No matter how trying the circumstances, if you can stay calm and reasonable, disaster can usually be averted.

Do not panic at mistakes. Audiences expect an occasional slip of the tongue. Simply correct yourself and go on. If they laugh at a blooper, laugh a little, yourself, wait for the noise to subside, and go on. If you miss a slide, forget it; the audience will never know.

Back To Aristotle

Remember that all the delivery techniques are just tools to help you reach the audience person-to-person. Choose your techniques with an eye to the means of persuasion. Use the tools that will help you establish a logical argument, convince the audience of your character, and put them in the right frame of mind.

Executive Summary

1. Delivery is more than a mechanical process. Doing and saying all the right things will not help unless you somehow touch the audience.

2. Have someone check your appearance before you go on.

3. Use common language, but beware of using locker-room words. A surprising number of people are offended by them.

4. Deliver part of your speech from one spot; then move on the transition and stop to deliver the next part.

5. Let your hands gesture as they would in conversation.

6. The most important aspect of eye contact is the feedback you get.

7. State one idea and watch the reactions. When the audience comprehends that idea, say another one.

8. Warm up your voice before an early morning speech.

9. Allow plenty of time to set up and adjust a microphone.

10. When time limits are important, let someone give you time cues.

13

Handling Visual Aids

In 1987, one of the hot topics at the International Technical Communication Conference was Computer Assisted Training, which made a breakout session on Computer Tutorials one of the hottest tickets at the conference. I got a seat early, which was smart; by the time the program started, the seating was standing room only. The program was delivered by two experts whose work put them at the leading edge of the field. Unfortunately, their communication expertise did not extend to the mundane matter of visual aid handling.

While one expert talked, the other sat beside the overhead projector to change slides. Every 15 or 20 minutes they would switch places. They had obviously rehearsed the program until the slide changes went like clockwork – but on a very slow clock! When it came time for the next transparency, the expert at the lectern would stop talking and nod to the expert at the overhead projector, who would nod back. She would then take the last slide off the projector, examine it by holding it up to the light, then study the stacks of slides on the projector table and carefully place the discarded slide in its assigned spot. She would then pick up another slide, hold it up to the light, carefully place it on the projector, glance at the screen, reposition the slide on the projector, glance again at the screen, make a minor adjustment, and finally nod again to the expert at the lectern, who would resume talking.

Watching this painstaking process would have been tolerable every five minutes or so – they were, after all, true experts in a vital field which most audience members knew little about. But they had dozens of slides, almost one for every sentence they spoke. The program was scheduled for an hour and twenty minutes. After thirty-five minutes, audience members started leaving. I was one of the tough ones who stuck it out. When the speakers finally finished, well over a quarter of the seats were empty.

I no longer remember what I learned about tutorials that day, but I will never forget what I learned about speaking – awkward or slow visual aid changes can sink even the brightest, most articulate speakers if they do not understand key concepts.

The Objectives

Ideally, visual aid handling should be so smooth and unobtrusive, the audience takes no notice of it and instead concentrates on the speaker's ideas. To achieve that end, the speaker must accomplish three objectives:

1. Control the audience's attention. When the speaker wants them to read the screen, they read the screen. When the speaker wants the audience to look at him, they look at him.

2. Maintain contact with the audience. As you recall, an audience must trust the speaker before they can be persuaded. Audiences do not relate to images on the screen; they relate to living human beings. If the speaker shows one image after another and depends on the visual aids to carry the presentation, the audience will receive a lot of information, but they are unlikely to be convinced.

3. Eliminate distractions. Any aspect of visual aid handling which draws attention to itself pulls that attention away from the speaker and the main ideas. In addition, certain types of distractions, such as obvious fumbling, look amateurish and endanger the speaker's credibility.

Methods for achieving these objectives vary depending on the type of equipment.

Working With an Overhead Projector

Learn how to operate the particular projector. It seems ironic that speakers should have trouble operating such a simple piece of equipment, but the various manufacturers of overhead projectors seem to have signed a pact that no two models will ever operate the same way. Consider the on-off switch. Depending on the make and model, you may encounter a slide switch, a rocker switch, a pushbutton, a wide bar (pushbar), or a toggle switch. The on-off switch may be on the front or on either side of the machine and is frequently clustered with other switches of the same type, all of which have minuscule labels. To complicate matters even more, every overhead I have seen has an adjustment knob on the upright post, but knobs which look the same can have different functions. Some of those knobs adjust the focus, while others raise and lower the image on the screen.

Have a backup. With every machine likely to be different, you need to take the time to check out all the controls. Remember to try switching to the secondary bulb. If the secondary bulb is burned out or missing, ask someone hosting the event to find a replacement. I have been astonished at the number of organizations which routinely put only one bulb in an overhead and have no replacements in the supply cabinet. Should you find yourself in that situation, try to find another overhead, so you can trade if a bulb blows. Failing in that, you need a contingency plan that will let you continue without visual aids.

Arrange the equipment and furniture. After testing the operation of the machine, determine where you will stand when changing overhead slides. Make sure you have enough table space on the correct side of the machine. Next, put a slide on the glass stage of the projector and size and focus the image. You may need to move the table up or back to get the correct size. To correct an image which appears skewed (side-to-side keystoning), rotate the base of the machine a few degrees clockwise or counter-clockwise. If the image is tilted even when the projector is on a level surface, usually the head is loose, or the arm or post holding the head is loose. You may be able to correct the tilted image by pushing one of these components back into alignment. Should that fail, the only quick fix is to prop up the projector's legs on one side. Incidentally, that wobbly misalignment is usually caused by carrying the projector by the upright post.

If others will use the machine before you, determine if the arrangement they favor will also work for you. I once saw a series of presentations with the overhead projector on a small, narrow table. The first presenter was a tall right-handed man. He moved the table so he had plenty of room to put down his slides. The next presenter was a short left-handed woman, who stood on the other side of the projector without making any adjustment. She only had room to place one stack of slides on her side of the table, which meant whenever she took a slide off the projector, she had no place to put it. She solved the problem by leaning in front of the projector to put the discarded slides on the other side. Each time she did it the projector beam hit her in the face and projected her silhouette on the screen.

When you are not the first speaker, you may need to recruit someone to help make the equipment shift, and you definitely need to mark the projector's location with masking tape on the table and the table's position with masking tape on the floor. Having the marks lets anyone put the equipment in place without having to fiddle with it.

Set the lights. Room lights are often on several circuits. Experiment to see what works best, remembering your intention is to have plenty of light on you without getting too much light on the screen. The choices will be easier to make if you have someone stand in for you while you watch from the back of the room. If the screen has a light directly overhead, anything projected on the screen will be washed out. Either move the screen or take out the light. All you have to do is climb a ladder and unscrew the bulb or fluorescent tube.

Mask the projector. The slides for each particular speech should have a consistent format, either vertical or horizontal. Having all the slides in one format makes them easier to handle, easier to store, and easier to mask. Most overhead projectors project a square image, but the transparencies are typically rectangular. For a more professional appearance, most presenters like to block or mask the stray light around the edges of the slide. To mask slides in frames, put one slide on the projector and watch the screen while moving the slide to the best possible position. Then check for a stray bar of light on either side, top, or bottom. If light is projecting outside the edges of the frame, use masking tape or freezer tape on the glass stage of the projector to block out the light. Do not leave this tape on the projector more than a week, or it will be hard to remove.

While you have the tape out, you can simplify your slide handling by taping stops on the projector at the top and one side of the frame. Some speakers tape down pencils for stops; I have had better luck taping down small plastic boxes such as aspirin or small breath mints come in. Some projectors come with small prongs, which fit into holes on the slide frames. If you have that system and the correct frames, you won't need to use masking tape or stops, but if you travel, you should take masking tape and stops just in case. With either prongs or stops in place, you do not need to look at the screen while changing slides. They will slip into the right spot consistently.

Putting the slides in flip-frames will simplify the masking, but you may still want to use stops.

At one point in my career, all the overhead slides I used were in cardboard frames, but I have come to prefer a transparency holder taped to the projector with the individual slides being unframed. Stores which stock audiovisual supplies usually sell transparency holders, but they are very easy to make, as described on page 96. Using a transparency holder makes a stack of slides very compact and saves time, both in preparing the slides and in setting up the projector.

Having an Assistant at the Overhead: You can either flip the overhead slides yourself or have an assistant sit by the projector and flip them. Having an assistant frees you to move around the room without the need to keep returning to the projector.

Because the assistant is seated, you may be able to place the projector lower, so it doesn't block the view of the audience. However, see the advice about keystoning and how to correct it in Chapter 7. If the room is equipped with a back projection screen, you can even put the projector and assistant in an adjacent room where the audience will not see them at all.

Having an assistant lets you concentrate on the speech without worrying about the details of changing slides, but, to use the assistant successfully, you will need some sort of signaling system (presumably, quicker and less conspicuous than the system used by the computer tutorial experts). Also, unless you have an unpaid volunteer, the assistant's salary will significantly increase the cost of a presentation.

Handling the Overhead Yourself: Changing the overhead slides yourself limits your freedom of movement, but totally eliminates the coordination problem.

An inexperienced speaker can kill a speech by having long unplanned pauses when changing slides. You should rehearse enough to be able to continue talking while manipulating slides. However, as soon as a new slide is on the screen, you should pause briefly to let the audience study it. If you plan to use a slide more than once in the same presentation, consider making a duplicate. That will save you from having to flip back through the stack of used slides to find the one you want.

Don't block the projector. Because you need to stand close to the projector while changing slides, you may get too close and cast a shadow on the screen. Most people who make this mistake are unaware of it; unless the projector beam hits you in the face, you are not likely to notice. The solution is to train yourself so you know how close is too close. Either rehearse with a video camera or get the rehearsal audience to tell you whenever they see your shadow on the screen.

Don't show a slide prematurely. Since any visual aid will attract the audience's attention, you should prevent the audience from viewing a slide when it would be distracting. Sometimes you want to go directly from one slide to another. At other times, you want to show one slide and then turn the audience's attention back to you and talk for awhile before showing the next slide. In other words, you want the screen dark for a time. Turn off the projector if you can do it quietly, or simply cover the slide with a file folder, or cover the projection lens with a file folder. If you cover the lens, try not to let the folder touch the lens itself. On some models, the glass lens gets hot enough to cause a file folder to smolder. The main advantage of covering the lens instead of the slide is that you can change slides while the screen is dark. An alternative for covering the lens is to tape a piece of paper, cardboard, or aluminum foil on the lens housing, so you can flip it down in front of the lens.

Avoid the blank, lighted screen. Whenever you remove one slide and don't immediately put another one up, the audience is confronted with a blank, lighted screen, which is distracting and also suggests you are not paying close attention. Avoiding this problem is very easy. Rehearse your slide changes so that when you see a slide change coming up, you get ready ahead of time. *While you are talking*, pick up the next slide with one hand. Hold that one and *keep talking* while you use your other hand to get a grip on the slide on the projector. Then, *as you talk*, simultaneously move one slide off and the other on. Lay the old slide face down on the stack of used slides and move aside so the audience can see the screen. This maneuver can be done with a note card or pointer in hand, but it is easier if you lay the card or pointer down.

Talk to the audience, not the screen. A common fault, even among experienced speakers, is to direct much of the presentation to the screen, rather than to the audience. It is appropriate to glance at the screen to see if the slide is correctly positioned, but then you must face the audience to talk about the slide. If you wish to point at something on the slide, you can do so either standing at the screen or standing at the overhead projector. In either case, you should not stare at the pointer, but should hold the point while turning your head to look at the audience.

Hold the pointer still. If you cannot keep the pointer steady, use a pen or pencil and lay it on the stage of the overhead projector pointing at the desired part of the slide. The swizzle sticks which some airlines provide can also be laid on a slide as pointers. Be careful not to fiddle with a big pointer when you are not using it. Either hold it motionless at your side or lay it down.

Let the audience see the screen. Imagine a line drawn from each audience member's nose to the edge of the screen. If you block that line, that person will not be able to see the whole screen. You will almost always block someone's view while you change slides, so you should move out of the way as soon as you can. If you use a swizzle stick or pencil as a pointer, position it, then move to the side or move back. Standing beside the screen will normally let you point out things without blocking any sight lines.

Working With a 35mm Projector

Make sure your slides and carousel are compatible. Ask your contact or liaison which types of carousels have worked in the past, bearing in mind that the only way to know for certain is to test all the components together. Be sure to check compatibility early enough to make any needed changes.

Learn how to operate the particular projector. Be sure you can find every control in the dark. Test everything, especially the remote, which seems to be a weak point in some designs. In case the remote gives trouble, you should know how to disconnect it and use the other controls. Rapidly run through the whole carousel to make sure every slide is right side up.

If possible, do your tests at the same time of day you will be speaking. Otherwise, you may be surprised by the difference in lighting intensity. (Your notes, which were easily read at noon are invisible at 8:00 P.M. The slides which were bright and colorful at night are washed out the next morning.)

You may have to recruit someone to control the room lights during your presentation. Anytime you want the audience to look at you instead of the screen, you must black out the screen, either by turning off the projector or inserting an opaque slide. Either way, when the room loses the reflected light from the screen, it will be very dark unless someone brings up the lights.

You should never use a slide without testing it under actual lighting conditions to see if it can be read from the back of the audience. If it can't, either drop it or change it.

Working With Flip Charts/Flip Cards

A flip chart is a pad of paper which is flipped one sheet at time. Flip cards are white poster board cards. Each system has its defenders who claim the other system is impossible to manipulate. Handle them both to find your preference. When using flip cards, start with the backs of the cards to the audience to avoid exposing information too early.

When using flip charts, hide information by leaving a blank page between written pages, or start with the sheets flipped over the top of the easel and pull them down one at a time, working from the last page to the first.

To make the paper sheets easier to flip, attach small masking tape tabs or fold-down (dogear) the corners. You should tab or dogear both sides of each page; you can't always predict which side of the easel you will be working from.

Working With Samples, Models, and Pictures

To avoid distracting the audience, you must keep objects out of sight unless they are being discussed. Place objects in a bag on the floor or cover them. Avoid passing objects among audience members. Instead, allow the audience to view the objects on the next break.

Avoidable Disasters

Unless you enjoy Russian roulette, you should *never* put slides or speech notes in checked baggage. Anything else you might lose to the luggage monster can be bought, rented, or borrowed on short notice. Notes and slides cannot.

Executive Summary

1. Awkward or slow visual aid changes can sink even the brightest, most articulate speakers if they do not understand key concepts.

2. In handling visual aids, a speaker has three objectives:

    a. Control the audience's attention.

    b. Maintain contact with the audience.

    c. Eliminate distractions.

3. The controls which operate overhead projectors vary greatly. Make sure you can operate the projector you will be using.

4. Plan in advance what you will do if the bulb burns out.

5. Experiment with the room lights to get plenty of light on you, but not too much on the screen.

6. Make all overhead slides for one presentation in the same format (vertical or horizontal).

7. Having an assistant change slides will let you concentrate on the presentation and will give you greater freedom of movement, but the assistant's salary will greatly increase the cost of the presentation.

8. If you will be handling the overhead slides, rehearse enough to be able to continue talking while changing the slides.

9. To avoid casting a shadow on the screen, stay out of the projector's beam.

10. If you want the screen dark for a time, turn off the projector if you can do so quietly, cover the slide with a file folder, or cover the projection lens with a file folder.

11. You can glance at the screen or point to the screen, but then you must turn back and talk to the audience.

12. If you cannot hold a pointer steady, take a pen, pencil, or swizzle stick and lay it on top of the transparency on the stage of the projector.

13. When using a 35mm projector, make sure your slides and carousel are compatible.

14. With either type projector, never use a slide without testing it first. See if it can be read from the farthest seat in the room.

15. When working with samples, models, or pictures, you should keep the objects out of sight until you are ready to discuss them. Place objects in a bag on the floor or cover them. Avoid passing objects among audience members. Instead, allow the audience to view the objects on the next break.

14

Answering Questions

Questions are valuable from a speaker's standpoint because they allow him to speak directly to the needs of the audience. Even the most thorough audience analysis only allows predictions of what the audience will do and say – and predictions can be wrong. You can only persuade people if you address their concerns, and every question tells you exactly what is on one person's mind at that moment. You no longer need to guess at what they would like to know.

Anticipating the Questions

If you have analyzed your audience well, you will be able to guess the content of most questions and the tone in which they will be asked. Any time you are unsure of what the audience will ask, you should consult with people who know them better, or convene a rehearsal audience which is similar in outlook to the real audience. Major politicians typically rehearse every news conference with staff members who ask every possible question. You may not have time for that sort of intensive preparation, but you should certainly think about the obvious questions and practice answering them.

Some speakers even hold some of their material in reserve. They prepare additional facts, examples, and visual aids which may be pressed into service during the Q & A session. I do that in my workshop on Dealing With Difficult People. Because of the title, many highly frustrated people attend. Most of these people work or live with someone who is difficult to the point of being infuriating.

During the workshop, we explore and practice distinguishing the different types of difficult behavior and responding to each particular type appropriately, thereby lessening the damage and nudging the difficult person toward change. Sometimes, in the middle of the day, one of the frustrated participants will explode.

> *I work with this guy who is a jerk. I mean an ABSOLUTE JERK! And I am already doing all the things you have told us to do, and THIS GUY IS STILL A JERK!*

At that point I smile and start telling this story, acting out the dramatic parts.

> *There was a soldier in the Korean War who lost his rifle. He went to the supply sergeant who told him they were out of rifles.*
>
> *"What am I gonna do?! There's gonna be a battle tomorrow!"*
>
> *Sergeant said, "just relax. The enemy we are fighting have lived all their lives in a totalitarian dictatorship. Which makes them very susceptible to the power of suggestion. Just hold your hands like this, like you're aiming a rifle, and say very resolutely, 'BANG! BANG!' It will have the same effect as if you shot a rifle."*
>
> *The soldier couldn't believe what he was hearing, but he didn't have a choice. There were no more rifles. He went out, then ran back in. "Wait a minute, I lost my bayonet too. What do I do if they get in close?"*
>
> *"Same principle. Hand-to-hand combat, just stick your fingers in front of you like this and go, 'STAB! STAB!'"*
>
> *Now the soldier was really freaked out, but he had no choice. Sure enough, next day the battle started and the enemy came pouring over the hill. He aimed his invisible rifle and went, "bang, bang," AND ONE OF THEM DROPPED! Then he went, "BANG! BANG! . . . BANG! BANG!" They kept dropping, but then he saw a giant coming toward him.*
>
> *The guy was huge, looked like a sumo wrestler. "BANG! BANG!" The giant kept coming. "BANG! BANG! . . . BANG! BANG!" Now he was in close. "STAB! STAB! . . . STAB! STAB!" Nothing worked. The giant knocked him*

down, walked over him, stepped on his face, and as he was going by he said, "TANK, TANK . . . TANK, TANK."

When the laughter subsides, I make my point: "Sometimes, even when you do everything right, nothing works. You can't force someone to change. But the actions we are practicing are still the best response because they limit the damage. You can be sure, if these tactics don't work, nothing else will work, either."

During or After the Speech?

Normally, either you or the moderator should tell the audience in advance whether questions should come during or after your speech. Taking questions during the speech is harder on you, but is likely to be more effective. A question during the speech allows you to clarify or emphasize an unclear point before people forget it. Interaction during the speech also keeps the audience's attention focused on your ideas. The only times I would suggest holding questions until the end is when protocol requires it or the speech is so tightly woven that any interruption would throw it off course.

Questions during the speech do create some problems, which you should be prepared for. An obvious problem is the need for you to keep track of where you are in your speech outline. You may want to slip a paper clip or the clip of your ball-point pen on your notecard to mark your place.

If someone raises a point you intended to cover later, you must decide whether to discuss it immediately or tell the audience it will come later. If the order of your points is basically arbitrary, you might as well talk about the one the audience is immediately concerned with. Just go ahead and give that part of your speech in advance. Some speakers prepare what is essentially a modular speech and then use the audience questions as cues to deliver whichever block is appropriate at the time. If the order of your points is not flexible, tell the audience you will cover that issue later – then be sure you do.

Questions during the speech also make it more difficult for you to keep track of time. You should know how much total time is allotted for the speech and questions, and you can mark your outline with the time it takes to deliver each essential block. If you see time running short, you can drop the non-essential blocks and, if necessary, stop the questioning firmly, but politely.

Encouraging Questions

Normally, you want the audience to ask questions. By doing so, they become more involved in the subject and they help you tailor your remarks to their particular needs. Unfortunately, many speakers unwittingly discourage questions. Sometimes a speaker will give an energetic, confident speech and then suddenly revert to a nervous, withdrawn posture for the questions. You should not slouch, look at the floor, or stand with your arms crossed or your hands clasped. Simply stand erect with your hands at your sides and look at the audience.

To encourage questions, you should step toward the audience, raise your hand, and say, "What questions do you have?" Then wait. Too many speakers hurry on without giving the audience time to organize their thoughts. By waiting, you tell the audience you expect a response. Usually, you will get one. Raising your hand can make the process more orderly. Audience members will probably follow suit, rather than simply yelling out questions.

When Answering

Recognize the questioner. If you know the questioner's name, say it. Otherwise, say something like, "the lady in the back."

Listen carefully to the question. This step is critical. You want to be sure you understand the question; you want to pick up any feelings or hidden agendas behind the question; and you want to continue to communicate that you are a person who is organized, confident, and in control of the situation.

Unless the questioner is hostile or incredibly long-winded, you should listen carefully to the entire question without interrupting. At the same time, you should try to get a sense of how the audience feels about the question, since your answer will be aimed at all of them. If you do not understand the question, say so and ask for a clarification.

Repeat the question. Even if the audience heard the original question clearly, repeating it is a good idea. By repeating the question, you gain several seconds to think about your answer and you reassure the questioner that you understood what was asked. Audiences will allow you to paraphrase instead of repeating the question word for word. Paraphrasing the question allows you to restate it in a form which is easier to handle. If the question is rambling, you can focus it. If it was hostile, you can soften or deflect it.

Do not preface your answer. "That's a very good question; I'm glad you asked it" is a tired cliché, long-overdue for retirement.

Use the questioner's name. Calling any audience member by name keeps the whole audience more alert and involved.

Address the questioner and the audience. You can't afford to concentrate only on the questioner if you expect to hold the audience. In fact, you may occasionally encounter an adversary who tries to sucker you with a series of difficult questions. If you take the bait, you will get drawn into a one-to-one conversation which loses the audience. You should regard every question as a question from the whole audience and divide your eye contact between the person who asked it and everyone else.

If the questioner is the only person concerned with at particular issue, consider answering privately on a break.

Don't bury the lead. The answer to a question needs to be as well organized as anything else you say. Every news reporter learns early that the lead for a story has to go up front. If the lead is buried in the middle somewhere, the readers may miss it. You should follow the same principle. Never get so caught up in the details of your answer that you forget the main point. As a general rule, you should state the main point first and then explain or defend it. If the answer is long, restate the main point at the end.

Hostile Questions

At first glance it may look like a speaker is an easy mark for any angry listener who wants to snipe at him, but actually the speaker has the advantage. The speaker is facing the audience and may have a microphone; whereas, a questioner may have trouble being seen and heard. The speaker or the moderator controls the flow of questions, so the hostile questioner cannot choose his timing. And the audience typically expects brief questions, which limits the questioner's ability to defend his position. Answers, on the other hand, can be brief or elaborate, as the speaker chooses. This is a significant advantage.

General defenses: If you know in advance who will try to nail you to the wall and you are addressing a fairly large audience, pick other people to ask questions. Depending on the type of meeting and your political skills, you may be able to plant some sympathetic questions to dilute the number of hostile ones.

If you don't know who will ask the tough questions, you will find out soon enough. In that case, remember who the tough guy is and don't give him a second shot. Simply call on other people until time expires.

The Manifesto Question: Sometimes an opponent will begin making a lengthy statement in lieu of a question. Here is how to cut him off. As soon as you recognize the subject of the manifesto, throw your opponent off balance: if you don't recognize the person, ask him to state his name and organization. If you do recognize him, call his name and ask him to restate the first part of the sentence (or the last part – but not the whole thing). Both tactics are designed to slow him down, to cause him to stop and think for a minute, which takes him out of his prepared statement. After he answers your interruption, it will take him a moment to collect his thoughts and get back into the prepared statement. But you jump on the pause and take back the initiative. Before the questioner can collect himself and resume the attack, rephrase the question, answer it briefly (Don't bury the lead!), and then ask for a question from another person. Thus, you leave the attacker without a platform from which to fire another volley.

Should he object out loud, you can turn the audience against him by pointing out politely that you have already answered one of his questions and you would like to hear the concerns of other audience members.

The accusation: ("Why have you overlooked the most cost-effective approach?") Stay calm and objective. Rephrase the question to soften it: "Have we missed the most cost-effective approach?" Include the whole audience in your answer; then move on.

The never-forget question: ("Why should we approve this renovation when you spent $700 for a plumbing fixture last year?") Don't get suckered into fighting past battles. Instead, shift back to your agenda. ("We have to evaluate this proposal on its own merits.")

The have-you-stopped-beating-your-wife question: ("Have you stopped sending out defective equipment?") A yes or no answer will trap you. Stay on the issue, but sidestep the question. ("Let me describe our quality control procedures to you. . . .")

Other Difficult Questions

The incomprehensible question: You have three options:

1. Ask the questioner to repeat it.

2. Rephrase it to a question you would like to answer.

3. Explain that the answer may be complicated and offer to answer it after the meeting. By talking back and forth with the questioner later, you should be able to glean the essence of the question.

The I-slept-through-it-all question: After you spend ten minutes explaining how software metrics can determine the relative complexity of different computer programs, someone pops up to ask if you have ever heard of something called software metrics? Much as you would like to, you can't afford to be condescending. Just give the simplest, briefest explanation you can think of and go on.

The off-the-point question: This one comes out of left field. You have been explaining how to put together a successful grant proposal when someone asks whether you think TV or direct mail is a better advertising medium. Be careful not to attack or embarrass the questioner. His credibility is already gone – don't send yours with it. If you can answer the question briefly, do so and go on. If you can't, explain that the question is important but about a different area.

The unexpected question: This is the one you don't expect and don't have an answer for. The answer you should give is simple: "I don't know, but I will find out and get back to you." Then be sure to follow up.

Questions From a Large Audience

The larger the audience the more difficult the question period becomes – regardless of whether the audience is friendly or hostile. As the audience approaches 500, both the speaker and the audience have trouble hearing the questions. Because the number of hands in the air is greater, people must wait much longer to be called on. Some will become impatient and yell their questions without being recognized. When that happens, the room is only one step from the sort of chaos that occurs when TV reporters mob an indicted politician leaving the courthouse.

A smart speaker who sees this problem coming will head it off at the pass. Adding additional microphones can help establish a sense of order. One method which works well in an auditorium is to have a person with a portable mike in each aisle. The moderator takes questions from each mike in turn; while one person is speaking in the right microphone, the keeper of the left mike hands it to the next questioner.

A variation on this approach has stationary mikes on stands, either on the corners of the stage or at the front of each aisle. Questioners line up behind each mike, and questions come from each mike alternately. To keep order, someone needs to stand by each mike and serve as a gatekeeper.

The other basic method for taking questions from a large group is to require written questions. If this concept is to work smoothly, the audience must have time to write the questions, and the organizers of the event need some efficient method for collecting them.

The process becomes simpler if the speech and question period are separated by a break. As the audience files out, ushers offer index cards to them. When the audience comes back in, the ushers collect the questions. Then someone must quickly sort the questions and pick the ones the speaker will address.

This sorting process will be less hectic if the questions are collected at the beginning of the lunch hour. Some groups use a committee to do the sorting, which lessens the chance someone will claim key questions were censored. If the audience is already divided into groups, they can be enlisted to sort the questions as they are written. The moderator simply asks each group to supply one or two questions *from the group*. In discussing possible questions, the audience groups usually drop or rewrite those which are wacky, nasty, or fuzzy.

Executive Summary

1. Letting the audience ask questions gives you a chance to hear their real concerns, which you must address in order to persuade them.

2. Consider holding some material in reserve to use in answering questions.

3. Listen carefully and repeat each question.

4. The speaker has the advantage over hostile questioners because the speaker can control the timing and choose the questioners.

5. With large crowds, use written questions.

15

When Things Go Wrong

Remember the two communication experts I described in Chapter 13, the ones who drove away their audience with time-lapse transparency changes. I returned to the International Technical Communication Conference the next year determined to strike a blow for better speaking. Bob Weaver and I were leading a workshop on presentation skills. We planned to alternate presenting different topics, then let the participants give impromptu speeches the first day and prepared speeches the second day. I was to start with a 45 minute block on mastering fear and gaining confidence, the same material as Chapter 1 of this book. I began with my best dramatic opening:

> *Did you know the number one fear of Americans is the fear of public speaking? A group of researchers asked 3,000 Americans what they were most afraid of and "speaking in public" led the list. The fear of death only tied for sixth place! (Good thing they didn't ask about the fear of death WHILE speaking.)*

At that moment a woman in the back of the room jumped to her feet.

> *Wait a minute! How old is your data?*

Suddenly, I was off track – where on earth could this question be leading?

I, uh, think the study was done in the 70's.

THEN IT'S NOT TRUE ANYMORE. THE NUMBER-ONE FEAR TODAY IS AIDS!

As soon as she said it, I knew she was right. For months, every scrap of information about AIDS had been front-page news. People seemed to think we would be engulfed by the epidemic like a rowboat in a typhoon. Immediately, two thoughts crossed my mind:

1. It's time to retire this speech.

2. How am I going to get through the next 45 minutes?

Everyone who gives very many briefings, presentations, or speeches will eventually have one where something goes wrong. Perhaps you are speaking in a hotel and the staff schedules your meeting in half of the ballroom at the same time rock musicians for the evening's heavy metal concert are setting up and testing their amplifiers in the ballroom's other half. (Which has happened to countless speakers.)

Perhaps a waitress at a formal banquet spills a plate of peas down your neck. (Which has happened to me.)

Perhaps your assistant, the most dependable person in the organization, puts some of the wrong slides in your carousel with half of them upside down. (As I have seen happen.)

Perhaps nervousness drives you to the restroom one last time before you go on and you deliver the speech with your shirt-tail hanging out your open fly.

Perhaps the microphone contracts a terminal illness. Several years ago I spoke to a retired men's club. I should say a RETIRED men's club. Many of these guys were so old their children had retired. We met in a room with poor acoustics and a sound system that sounded like a lion with bronchitis – anything said into the mike came out as a choppy growl. The chairman called the meeting to order, "Argh, argh, ark-ark, worra-worra," and throughout the audience I could see men whispering to each other. ("What did he say?" "Beats me.") The more alert audience members began adjusting their hearing aids. Then the secretary read the minutes of the last meeting, "Arka-ark-ark, arghhh." ("What's he saying?" "I dunno.")

Finally, I was introduced, ''Worff, ark-ark-ark, worra-worff.'' (''Who's that young guy?'' ''Beats me.'') The fact that the audience couldn't hear my introduction turned out to be a blessing since the program chairman seemed to invent a new biography for me while staring at the introduction I had written. (He told me after the meeting he was going in that week to have cataract surgery on both eyes.)

I have always felt whatever other merits a speech may have, if the audience cannot hear it clearly, it is worthless. There was no time to inquire about another mike; the president and the program chairman had each told me individually they were on a tight schedule. I would not be allowed even a minute over my allotted time.

I knew that orators from Cicero to William Jennings Bryan managed to get their points across without the aid of sound equipment, and some of them must have worked in rooms with poor acoustics. I stood up, smiled, moved the microphone where it could do no harm, and yelled at the top of my lungs, ''CAN YOU HEAR ME IF I TALK LIKE THIS?'' Half the audience nodded.

The speech rapidly fell into a pattern. I would yell ten words or less, wait while the echo died away, watch while the half of the audience with better hearing repeated what I said to the others, then yell another ten words. To stay on schedule, I had to throw out half of my material, which was okay with me. The yell-wait-wait-yell routine would have destroyed the timing on all the funny parts, anyway.

Keep Rolling

You can survive anything which goes wrong as long as you keep your head. Audiences are amazingly inattentive; major problems will often pass unnoticed. Several years ago, I gave some public seminars in New Zealand. I had requested a cordless lapel mike, but the hotel in Auckland furnished a lapel mike with 100 feet of electrical cable attached. At that time, I understood in theory how to work with a lapel mike and cable, but had almost no practical experience with one. I passed the cable through the back of my suspenders, where my coat would hide it, shoved the metal connector (which hooked the short mike lead into the long cable) in my front pocket and clipped the lapel mike on my tie. The system projected my voice loud and clear, and, by keeping an eye on the cable, I was able to avoid tripping on it or getting it snagged on a table leg. The seminar was on presentation skills; after explaining a four-step method for creating an impromptu speech,

I invited anyone in the audience to give it a try. A woman in the middle of the crowd accepted. For her to be heard, I had to pass her the mike, so I unclipped it from my lapel, pulled up slack through my suspenders, and passed the mike down the row of spectators.

When she finished speaking, they handed the mike and ten feet of cable back to me. Getting rid of the excess cable seemed easy enough; while I continued talking I would reach back and pull the excess cable back through my suspenders – simple. As I kept talking with eye contact focused on the audience, the process of pulling out the slack seemed to take longer than expected. Eventually, after it seemed I had been pulling out slack forever, I glanced down at my feet. Thirty feet of tangled cable lay in a mass before me – I had been pulling on the wrong side of the loop through my suspenders! I looked at the audience; three people directly in front of me were chuckling over my predicament, but no one else had noticed. So I stopped fiddling with the cable and continued talking for another half hour, kicking the mass of cable in front of me each time I moved, until we reached a scheduled break time. During that half hour, with the cable tangled at my feet, no one else caught on.

This incident illustrates the first principle of dealing with a problem while speaking:

> If the audience is not aware of the problem, minimize the damage and go on without mentioning it.

Because the audience's attention normally goes wherever you direct it, if you show no signs of alarm and keep their attention elsewhere, they won't realize anything is wrong.

Now, let's consider the second principle of dealing with a problem while speaking:

> The audience will ignore small mistakes unless the speaker magnifies them.

I once saw a woman give a solid, convincing speech, but afterward, during the question and answer session, she suddenly exclaimed, ''My slides! I forgot all about my slides!'' A moment before she had no problem – now she had convinced the audience something was seriously wrong. Most speakers are less dramatic than she was, but many otherwise good speakers have the bad habit of apologizing whenever something goes wrong.

''It's really too bad about the projector breaking. I mean,

*this speech loses most of its impact without slides. Some of
them are really beautiful, but, well, here goes.''*

If the speech is doomed to fail without slides, don't give it. If you can
make it work without slides, give it that way without apology. Above all,
don't coach the audience to expect a failure.

The emotional effect of speaking problems can range from slightly
embarrassing to devastating. Whether the effect is mild or severe, your
response should be the same: control the situation, limit the damage, shift
the audience's attention away, and go on. In the slightly embarrassing
category, I would put my unfortunate habit of knocking over other people's
water glasses when I talk. Sometimes, I am lucky and the tablecloth soaks
up all the water. In those cases, I set the glass upright and continue without
comment. When I am unlucky, the waters spills on a person or on someone's notes. In those cases, I do what I can to help mop up the water, laugh
with the audience if they are laughing, and then go on. On the next break, I
will go back to the person who got wet and apologize.

At the other end of the emotional scale are truly disturbing experiences,
which may be funny later, but are genuinely painful at the time.

The Worst Thing That Ever Happened

When professional speakers get together casually, they often trade
stories about "the worst thing that ever happened to me." Since three
typical professional speakers will have trouble fitting all their egos into one
medium-sized room, a sort of one-upsmanship frequently develops. I can
usually one-up with the best of them by relating the following incident.

I once offered a workshop through the Colorado Free University. I
came early, got everything set up, cheerfully met people at the door, and
helped them through a fairly complicated registration procedure. As usual,
half the class showed up ten minutes before starting time. At two minutes
before starting time, I looked at the next person in line and recognized my
ex-wife, who I had not heard from in eight years. I knew I should speak, but
my mouth refused to move; finally, I said, "This is a surprise."

She giggled, "Um hum."

At that moment, my mind seemed to split in two. Half of me was
talking her through the mechanics of registration:

"I need to collect your registration voucher and a check for the registration fee. Then you can make a name tag and pick up one of . . ."

The other half of my brain was approaching escape velocity.

What does she want? My skin is on fire! How'd she get a new last name? I'm going to have fever blisters over my whole body! How can I talk when I can't even swallow? How can I walk when the room keeps spinning?

More than anything in my whole life, I wanted to go down to the men's room, splash cold water on my face, do a breathing exercise, and collect my wits. The audience wouldn't care if we started two minutes late – but somehow she would know exactly what I was doing! I remembered my Uncle Bob Murphy's warning about New Orleans traffic: "Don't look back, cause they'll take it as a sign of fear."

I took a deep breath, wobbled to the front of the room, and started talking. She was on my right, so I concentrated on the audience on my left. Something must have worked – they were laughing in all the right places. Eventually I sneaked a glance to my right. She was beaming. I opened up and did the program as I always did, except that I stuck in two pointed references to my present wife and deleted some material about my ex-wife's mother. When it was over, the critiques were all favorable. Her's was glowing and she printed her phone number at the bottom. I didn't call.

By the way, the class was on Dealing With Difficult People.

Believe it or not, some speakers can top this story. One professional speaker told me he was sitting in his hotel room reviewing the keynote address he would give the next day when the meeting planner who had hired him to speak called. In a thinly disguised, but very suggestive, voice he offered a romantic evening – just the two of them. The speaker refused, but remembering the meeting planner would be on the front row for his keynote, he couldn't sleep. The next morning he took his bags down early and gave a cabby a big tip to take them to the airport and check them. Before the meeting started, he tracked down the meeting planner and asked for his check in advance.

"I was expecting to give it to you right after the speech."

"You don't understand. I will not step on the stage without that check in my pocket."

Finally, he got the check and proceeded to give the worst speech of his career, after which he ducked out the back entrance before anyone could catch him.

The bottom line is: NO MATTER WHAT HAPPENS YOU CAN GET THROUGH IT!

Executive Summary

1. Whatever goes wrong, never coach the audience to expect a failure.

2. Whatever goes wrong, keep going – the audience rarely catches on.

16

Staying in Practice

Public speaking is like dieting: if you don't stay with it, you end up back where you started. Remember speaking involves physical as well as mental skills. Giving a speech after a long layoff is like playing basketball after a long layoff: you are certain to feel awkward and rusty.

It would be far better to maintain your skills by giving speeches periodically. Frequent speaking can be an enjoyable challenge as you learn to turn nervous energy into the exhilaration of being in the spotlight.

If you are not already giving frequent speeches, you will need some way to develop speaking opportunities. The most obvious place to look is at your job. Volunteering to brief the workers or to talk to visitors or to represent your shop at a higher level staff meeting – all are good ways to show your talents to the people above you. Giving a speech always involves risk, of course, but, by remembering the principles you have learned, giving yourself plenty of time to prepare, and rehearsing with maximum simulation, you should be able to handle any speech you attempt.

If you can't get enough practice on the job, look elsewhere. Any metropolitan area offers dozens of opportunities for you to hone the speaking skills you need at work.

Two of the best sources for continued training and practice are Toastmasters and International Training in Communication (ITC). Both groups operate under similar formats (and, in fact, ITC was known as International Toastmistress Clubs until quite recently).

Both groups organize local clubs composed of men and women like yourself who want additional training and practice in speaking and other leadership skills. Members are generally very supportive and welcome newcomers. As with any decentralized organization, the style and effectiveness of individual clubs varies. Check out several before joining. To get information on clubs in your area or to find out how to organize a new club, contact:

Toastmasters International
P.O. Box 9052
Mission Viejo, CA 92690
Phone: 714/858-8255
Fax: 714/858-1207

International Training in Communication
P.O. Box 4249
Anaheim, CA 92803
Phone: 714/995-3660
Fax: 714/995-6974

A second approach is to look for speaking opportunities in the groups you already belong to and to offer your services to other groups looking for speakers. You could offer to:

Teach a class at your church.

Talk about your work to the Cub Scouts, Campfire Girls, Indian Guides, Indian Princesses, etc.

Speak to your local high school or junior high about substance abuse, motivation, safety, citizenship, etc.

Promote your favorite charity to any group who will listen.

Demonstrate your favorite hobby to any interested group.

Teach a credit or continuing education course on nights or weekends at your local community college.

Take a leadership role in your professional organization.

Volunteer as a guide at local tourist attractions.

In addition, there are surely dozens of groups in your area whose weekly or monthly programs are almost always speeches. In addition to service and civic clubs, such as Optimist, Kiwanis, Lions, Rotary and others, there are professional associations for every profession; alumni groups for various institutions; hobby clubs for everything from flowers to steam tractors; support groups for non-profit organizations; support groups for various other needs (single parents, relatives of Alzheimer's patients, etc.); and religious groups which span the spectrum.

Almost every one of these groups will have a program chairman who is desperately searching for something to do the month after next. If you reflect on your own job, hobbies, interests, and background, you are likely to discover several possible speech topics. By making yourself available to one of those desperate program chairmen, you are likely to get a free meal, meet some nice people, and possibly make some professional contacts.

Most speakers for clubs try to work up one good speech at a time and then deliver it over and over.

Should you find yourself developing cold feet instead of developing your speech, remember that local clubs do not normally have national celebrities as speakers. They have ordinary people like you and me talking about things that interest them.

After you have the speech outlined, you are ready to generate your own invitations. If you know some program chairmen, simply call them. If you don't know any, call the Chamber of Commerce and ask for a list of clubs and associations in your area. In some cities, the Chamber operates what is often called the *Presidents Club*, composed of the presidents of all the other clubs in town. A primary function of the Presidents Club is to trade information about local speakers. By talking to the president of the Presidents Club, you may be able to get five minutes on their program to introduce yourself and what you can offer.

You may prefer to talk to Cub Scouts, or you may prefer Kiwanians, but if you prefer not to talk at all, remember that speaking is a lot like downhill skiing. You can't conquer your fear of the mountain by staying in the clubhouse.

Executive Summary

1. Speaking skills get rusty during a layoff just as other complex physical/mental skills do.

2. If you are not giving frequent speeches, figure out a way to do so. Volunteer for any suitable occasion that comes along and seek out speaking opportunities.

17

The Media Monster

Suppose one morning your assistant said, "Barbara Walters is on line one. She wants to interview you for her 20/20 show – something about our environmental practices."

Of all the types of presentations a manager or executive is likely to give, none generates more anxiety than a media interview. Uncurbed anxiety can turn an otherwise amiable interview into a confrontation or make an otherwise competent manager or executive look sneaky and evasive.

The Al Campanis Bobble

A mishandled question can be deadly. On April 6, 1987, Al Campanis, the vice president for player personnel of the Los Angeles Dodgers was interviewed by Ted Koppel on ABC's Nightline concerning Campanis' forty-one-year friendship with Jackie Robinson. The interview preceded by nine days the fortieth anniversary of Jackie Robinson's debut as the first black major league baseball player. Early in the interview, Koppel asked why there were no black managers, general managers, or owners in the major leagues. Al Campanis' answer cost him his job.

Initially, Campanis said, "they may not have some of the necessities . . ." Responding to follow-up questions, he blundered from one stereotype to another. "Why are black men or black people not good swimmers? Because they don't have the buoyancy." After a commercial break, Koppel gave him a chance to "dig himself out," but he dug himself in deeper.

I have never said that blacks are not intelligent. I think many of them are highly intelligent. But they may not have the desire to be in the front office . . . But they're outstanding athletes, very God-gifted, and they're wonderful people. "[19]

Whether Campanis is racist or whether (as his friends claim) his off-the-cuff remarks do not reflect his true sentiments, the moral of the story is painfully obvious: If you don't know the answer, don't fake it!

While you may never face such dramatic consequences, what you say and how you say it to the media will typically have a definite impact on the public image of your organization. Just as the creation of firearms destroyed the knights' monopoly on military power, the creation of electronic media has destroyed the CEO's monopoly on image formation. The public perception of an organization is affected more by a shop foreman talking in front of a camera than by the president behind his desk.

Media Anxiety

Coping with media anxiety is no different in principle from coping with normal speech anxiety. You study the situation thoroughly, prepare well, and use your elevated nervous energy to increase your alertness and enthusiasm.

The Role Of the Media

In studying the situation, you need to understand the role of the news media. Leaders in business and government often assume reporters are out to get them. After all, didn't the paper report our organization's volunteer service work on page twelve, while the equal opportunity lawsuit was front-page news? Actually, the reason the bad news went on page one and the good news on page twelve has nothing to do with the newspaper's bias.

A journalist is in business to sell information; and the more dramatic the information, the better it sells. When was the last time you read the stuff on page twelve before the headlines on page one? Good new does make the front page if it is dramatic ("Last Minute Negotiations Avert Strike", "Workers Fight Exhaustion to Rescue Child").

The journalists you encounter will be looking for all sorts of information, good and bad, but their ears will be cocked for information that is dramatic.

Why Not Duck?

Since media interviews have the potential to do so much harm, why not just refuse them? A reporter can never force you to talk, so stone walling is always an option. Usually, it is a poor option, though. Every interview offers you a chance to build your company's image in the community. Even if your organization is under attack, you should normally agree to an interview so you can tell your side to the public. Little good can come from an announcer intoning, "company spokesmen have refused to speak to our reporter," and then handing the microphone to your opponent.

That is not to say you should agree to talk under any circumstances. You have an absolute right to silence with a corollary right to choose who you will talk with. You should politely insist on knowing who the interviewer is and who he or she represents. Jimmy Carter's admission that he had lusted in his heart would hardly have been news had he spoken it to the *Christian Science Monitor*. Saying it to *Playboy*, on the other hand, guaranteed it would haunt him for months.

You also have an absolute right to have the ground rules spelled out. The arrangement may not be pleasant, but it should be fair. The ground rules could include an agreement on off-the-record comments, but you would be better off not to say anything you do not wish repeated.

Ducking an interview would be the better part of wisdom if you are exhausted or unprepared. You should reschedule for the next day rather than jumping in over your head and risking disaster.

Your Role

Your job in an interview or press conference is to explain the good news clearly with as much energy as possible and to explain the bad news as simply as you can without adding to its dramatic appeal. So far as possible, you should make the good news seem dramatic and the bad news seem dull.

Even though you want to explain your organization's position as simply as you can, you should not resort to stereotypes or clichés.

Obvious Questions

Because anyone in a position of importance is likely to be interviewed eventually, you should prepare now for a spur-of-the-moment encounter with a journalist. You can't predict with certainty when someone will ask for an interview, and you can't predict every question. But you can predict the obvious questions because they are asked so often. Every executive and manager needs to be constantly prepared with simple, well organized answers to these basic questions:

What does your organization do?

How does your organization help the community?

How does your organization treat minorities and women?

A simple, well organized answer is one your grandparents or your car mechanic would understand.

Aggressive Questions

For some of you, the task is more difficult. The institutional values held by certain organizations are at variance with the values held by other segments of the public. If you work for an organization which is distrusted by a significant number of people, you need to think out what you will say in answer to aggressive questions. Consider these samples:

To the tobacco industry: Why do you continue running advertising which is clearly aimed at young people?

To the oil industry: Why is it that when OPEC prices rise, gasoline prices rise dramatically, but when OPEC prices fall, gasoline prices only drop slightly?

To the military: Why do you insist on gold plating weapon systems when the Cold War is over and the federal deficit is at record levels?

Clearly, this is not an exhaustive list. Any representative of one of these industries will face other tough questions, and other organizations will be forced to cope with other issues. Whatever the question, your chances of fielding it well will improve if you can anticipate the question and practice your answer. It should be equally obvious that you must thoroughly understand your organization's position on every issue which is likely to arise.

Anticipating the Questions

Before every presidential press conference, the President will spend hours with his advisors, rehearsing answers to every possible question. If you have a full-blown news conference scheduled, you should follow the President's example and have a full-blown rehearsal. If you have merely granted a five-minute interview in your office, you need not prepare so elaborately, but, at the very least, you should jot down expected questions and outline your answers.

But how do you predict the questions?

1. When the interviewer calls to set up an appointment, ask what you will be discussing.

2. Imagine yourself as a journalist trying to find something interesting and newsworthy in a supposedly dull interview. What sensitive areas would you seek out?

3. Ask your friends what concerns or questions they have about your organization. (Remember, the journalist will ask what he or she thinks the average person wants to know.)

4. Ask your boss, your coworkers, your subordinates.

5. Ask your spouse.

6. Read the Letters to the Editor column in your local newspaper. Even if the comments about your organization are exaggerated or inaccurate, they are likely to indicate concerns which you may be asked to address.

Having an Agenda

You should also have in mind the points you would like to make. You should not appear heavy-handed in twisting the conversation to your ends, but an open-ended question like "Would you care to comment on X?" gives you a golden opportunity to tell your side to the audience. Other opportunities may arise. If you notice a connection between a topic under discussion and a point on your agenda, bridge between them: "That brings up another important point. . ."

Most interviewers come with only a few prepared questions. After those are gone, each impromptu question will tend to relate to the answer you just gave. That means, if you can successfully bridge to your agenda, it may become the focus of the interview.

Come prepared with simple hard facts which are readily defensible. The judicious use of facts can go a long way toward keeping the press and the audience interested.

Personal Appearance

If you expect to face a still or video camera, have someone else check your appearance. Small things, like a missing button or a loose thread, things the audience wouldn't notice during a normal speech, can be glaringly obvious in a television closeup. Watching yourself on the evening news is not the time to discover that spot of barbecue sauce from lunch.

You should wear conventional clothes for your profession. To the audience at home, you are the company (or the government), so this is not the time to show off your Cher gown or Michael Jackson pants.

If you know where the interview will be, wear something which will present a pleasant color contrast to the background. Wearing the same color as the background is a good camouflage technique, but bad for projecting an image. You don't want to be invisible. You should also avoid any garment which has small contrasting stripes which are closely spaced. Bright red pin stripes closely spaced on a white background, for instance, will shimmer on the television screen, an effect which is very distracting.

On-Camera Behavior

You will have a more difficult time building trust with the television audience than with a normal audience. The television audience will typically see you for only short periods of time (due to camera shifts and editing) and some of them may be distracted by other things going on in their homes at the time of the broadcast.

For that reason, you should think about your behavior in front of the camera to maximize your chances of bonding with the audience. A television audience sees you at close range, so small things matter. Your posture should be straight, but relaxed; you must avoid overt fidgeting; and, above all, you must avoid furtive glances around the room. If the interviewer is talking, look at her. If you are talking, either look at the interviewer or talk to the audience by establishing eye contact with the camera lens. It may help to imagine the face of someone you know well positioned on the camera lens.

If you are in a studio with more than one camera, the one with a glowing red light is on-line. But be alert for the light to shift.

Despite the fact that some shows are seen by millions of people at once, television is an intimate medium. The typical viewer is not aware of the millions of other viewers, only the few who are in the room with him. When you face the camera, what you are doing, in effect, is having a conversation with two or three other people, and your style should reflect that. You need to be forceful and energetic, but you don't need to enlarge your voice and gestures as you would on a stage before a large audience.

Your body language should support your image as an alert, interested, confident individual in control of the situation. As you talk, lean forward slightly. As you listen, avoid obvious withdrawal signals such as crossing your arms. Study the behavior of network news commentators and network talk show hosts. Most of them have mastered the art of looking natural on camera.

Addressing Basic Concerns

You should never forget that the interviewer is not the ultimate audience. You are talking through the interviewer to the person on the street. Ordinary people are not greatly interested in the complexities of your operation. Whatever questions you face, remember that the concerns behind most questions are very basic. Do not get so caught up in the particulars of a question that you forget to answer the concerns.

Imagine for a moment that your organization has been transporting hazardous chemicals in railway tank cars. One of the cars has derailed and ruptured. No one was injured in the accident, and cleanup is proceeding, although very slowly because of the hazards.

You can expect to be asked several obvious questions: Who is responsible? Is the spill contained? Will it happen again? What are you doing to remedy the problem? In hearing your answers, the local audience is not especially interested in hearing that your people are working around the clock to solve the problem (although that is worth mentioning). They are not especially interested in hearing how many years you have transported chemicals without an accident (sounds like complacency), or how your industry cannot function without transporting dangerous substances (your problem, not theirs).

What they are interested in hearing is very basic, but critical to your image. Whatever you say about the particular issues, you must address the primary concern of local citizens: Are our families safe? In a crisis, whether real or perceived, people do not want to see an expert display his erudition. They want straight answers from someone who cares.

Too often, representatives of a company or government agency forget this principle in a situation like the hypothetical chemical spill and present their case to the media by discussing the exact composition of the chemical compounds and their critical importance to their organization. In such a situation, the public can hardly be blamed for assuming the organization cares more about the accuracy of its formulas than the safety of its neighbors. Say it again: *The public wants straight answers from someone who cares!*

Controlling the Tone

The television audience picks up impressions more readily than facts. You want to come across as calm, positive, and friendly, even if an occasional unscrupulous reporter tries to goad you into an explosion. Even if you flatten him with a perfect verbal counterattack, he will still win because of his editing power. He can always cut out your remarks or add his own clincher.

Avoid pouring gasoline on a raging fire. You can gain more from agreeing with the reporter's (and the audience's) concerns and responding with an item from your own agenda: "Well, George, I would like to ensure my family has clean air to breathe, too. What we have been doing along those lines is . . ." When the antagonist realizes every needling question of his merely gives you another chance to score a positive point, he will quit.

You should come across as fair, but being fair does not mean being verbose. In an attempt to be fair, a manager or executive may give a television audience the sort of full-blown explanation more appropriate to a staff analysis. In covering all possible aspects, citing all available statistics and studies, giving all possible qualifications, and covering all possible negative implications, you don't come across as fair – you come across as obscure! To win on television, you need to give well-focused answers of 45 seconds or less. You can do it – if you state your main point clearly in the first or second sentence of your answer and then follow up with clear support.

Practice

If possible, dry-run your media presentation using role playing. Have your colleagues toss you all the tough questions they can think of. Work on your answers until you can give a polished, concise reply to every question. After a tough practice session, you can gain a great deal of satisfaction in the actual interview by giving an easy answer to the question your interviewer thought was a stumper.

The Danger Zone

The hostile, but predictable, question presents less of a problem than the neutral, but totally unexpected, question. Consider Al Campanis again. Here is Campanis' explanation of the comments which ended his career:

> *I was dead tired after traveling when I went on the Nightline show. I got confused . . . I didn't want to go on. I was sitting in a seat in the empty Houston Stadium with a thing in my ear to hear the questions. I just wasn't myself. I got burned. I said things I didn't mean, explaining things I couldn't.*[20]

A successful media interview is likely to require all of your faculties and 100 percent concentration. Even before the question which tripped him, Campanis faced significant difficulties which ensured he would not be at his best.

1. He was "dead tired" and probably had jet lag.

2. He was inexperienced in dealing with national media.

3. He was in an unfamiliar setting with limited feedback, "sitting in a seat in the empty Houston Stadium, with a thing in my ear." Unable to see the interviewer or the audience, he lacked the visual feedback which would have shown him how shocking his comments actually were.

With rare exceptions, you should not accept an interview when you are unusually burdened by pressure or fatigue. Reschedule for a better time. Whenever the interviewer suggests arrangements you are not comfortable with, negotiate for a better setting.

But the biggest danger facing Campanis was not fatigue or the "thing" in his ear, but the unexpected question. I suspect he was anticipating questions about his early friendship with Jackie Robinson ("When you were helping him with technique, did you realize he had Hall of Fame potential?" – that sort of thing). In discussing his remarks several days later, Campanis said, "It was supposed to be a eulogy to Jackie Robinson. That's why I went on the program."[21]

Koppel's question came in an area where Campanis had very little information. He had been with the Dodger organization since 1943; while he may have understood why the Dodgers did not have a black manager or general manager, he was unlikely to know the reasons behind other teams' failure to hire blacks for managerial positions. Whether Al Campanis was a closet racist or completely color blind or somewhere in between, his best answer would be the same:

That's very regrettable, but I don't know the answer.

Shakespeare's Falstaff was right when he said, "The better part of valor is discretion."[22] Real heroes sometimes die in battle; they do not fall on their own swords by accident. When you get hit by a question which seems to come from some alternate universe, don't try to be heroic by speculating on the answer. The best response is very simple:

I don't know, but I will look it up and get back to you.

Executive Summary

1. Basic preparation for a media interview should start now – before you get called for an interview.

2. Managers should always be ready to answer basic questions about how their organization contributes to the community.

3. You have a right to fair ground rules in an interview. Ask the interviewer to spell them out in advance.

4. Avoid clothing that will fade into the background on television.

5. Talk to the television camera as if you were having a relaxed conversation with two or three people.

6. Always address the public concerns behind the questions.

7. Do not give complicated answers.

8. If you do not know an answer, say so. Never wing it.

18

Speaking Impromptu

The Impromptu Crisis

Picture this situation. You are sitting in another boring staff meeting, wondering when it will be over. This one is just like every other staff meeting except that all the top brass are present. As the meeting winds down to the does-anybody-have-anything-else? stage, you slide your notes back in your briefcase, ready for a quick departure. Suddenly, without warning, your boss turns to you and says,

> *Would you mind taking five minutes to tell us about that project you've been working on?*

At that point you have several choices:

Strangle your boss in front of the senior staff.

Catch your boss later and strangle him privately.

Resign.

Threaten to resign.

Talk.

If, in a situation such as this, you choose to talk, this section can be of some help. Giving a speech is somewhat like changing a diaper. There are times when it can't be put off.

Impromptu Occasions

Any time you must stand on your feet and talk with little or no preparation, you are giving an impromptu speech. Accomplished politicians can become quite skilled at impromptu speaking because of their numerous opportunities for off-the-cuff remarks. Even if you have no yearning for political life, you will not lack for impromptu opportunities. Consider the possibilities:

> Your boss has planned to represent your organization to visiting VIPs but becomes sick at the last minute. You must fill in to brief your organization's mission.

> You return from vacation to find the budget meeting has been moved up two weeks to this morning. Your assistant hands you the figures to talk from as you head for the meeting.

> Your service club is about to adopt an utterly stupid proposal. You see the flaws in the idea, but to explain them you will have to go to the front and use the microphone.

> The anchor woman from the evening news drops by. They have time for an extra story tonight, so they would like to shoot some footage around your work area and let you explain how your organization fits into the community. Sure, it's short notice, but your boss sent them to you because you handle short deadlines so well.

You can, I am sure, supplement this short list with other situations you have faced or might face. The common thread in each of them is the need to stand up and speak without advance preparation. Each situation is scary, but if you can stay organized and deliver a short, effective speech, you will rapidly become known as a clutch player, a decisive quick-thinker. But how do you pull it off?

The Four-Step Impromptu Technique

Every good impromptu speaker follows a simple system for organizing on the spur of the moment. Some systems are homemade; others are borrowed. The technique I favor was shown to me by Chuck Miller, former Director of Forensics at the Air Force Academy.

Chuck's technique has four steps, which are short enough to be easily memorized:

1. Main Point

2. Support

3. Opening

4. Closing

These steps are arranged in order of priority, the order in which you will think of them, not the order in which you will say them.

Let's see how the technique works in practice. You remember the first situation, the one your boss springs on you at the end of the staff meeting. With all the organization's heavyweights watching, you are supposed to talk about the new project for five minutes. You consider strangling your boss or resigning before finally deciding to talk. What then?

First, try to buy time. Rather than briefing from your seat, rise slowly, smile, straighten your coat or skirt, collect your notes, and walk deliberately to the lectern. This activity will gain the audience's attention, demonstrate that you are in control, and most important, give you a few seconds to think.

What you should think about is the four-step technique.

Main Point: In the normal process of speech preparation, you would be reviewing all the material you have gathered, searching for the one point which can serve as a unifying principle for the speech. In an impromptu situation, you don't have time to review everything you know about the subject. Instead, you must search your mind for one plausible point you can make about the subject. You are not searching for the best possible point to make; you want to take the first point you can think of which will work.

In our example, you were to brief on the status of the new project.

Let's suppose the project is a headache because it has fallen behind schedule. If you take "The project is behind schedule" as your main point, you will be barraged with questions. Try to forestall the questions by being more specific. Possible main points include:

We have been delayed because of late deliveries, but switching suppliers has solved the problem.

Lack of trained personnel has thrown us behind, but we are slowly catching up.

Lack of trained personnel has thrown us behind; we need more resources to catch up.

We have fallen behind, but quality remains high. We should continue current practices.

We have fallen behind because of unexpected technical problems, which suggests we should re-evaluate the project.

As soon as you have a workable main point, go to step two.

Support: You are now looking for two or three items which will directly support your main point. As before, you are not looking for the best possible solutions, but the first things that come to mind which will work. Suppose your main point is: We need more trained personnel to catch up. Supporting points might include:

The last project of this size had 60% more full-time workers.

We tried borrowing other people part-time, but other managers in the organization could not afford to spare them.

We have used Job Corps temporaries as far as possible, but some parts of the project require expertise they don't have.

We were only ten days behind on the first milestone, but we are now over three weeks behind.

There are other points you could make, but each of the preceding do support your main point and you already know enough to explain each of them. You now decide to lock in the supporting points. You should always try to arrange support in a meaningful pattern as you would in a rehearsed speech.

Opening: An impromptu opening has the same requirements as other speech openings. You need to capture the audience's attention and lead into the subject. Anecdotes work well. If the audience does not know you, you should probably introduce yourself. As with the main point and support, an opening need not be perfect. Take the first thing you can think of which will work. For our example, you could try a variation of the old "good news/bad news" routine:

> *The good news is we know exactly where we are on the project. The bad news is we aren't where we want to be.*

Closing: Just like any other speech: summarize the main points; call for action; and leave the audience with a clever tag line if you can think of one. Or just tie things up:

> *The bad new is we are slipping behind. The good news is it's curable. If we get the people, we can finish on time.*

Time Pressure

Is it possible to plan a speech completely as you walk to the front of the room? Sometimes. Remember, you will frequently be talking about something you are familiar with, and the extra adrenalin should give you an extra measure of mental agility. You may be surprised at the speed with which you can put a speech together when the pressure is on.

If you can't organize completely, remember the four-step technique is arranged in priority order. The first step, selecting a main point, is mandatory. If you get to the lectern before you have thought of a main point, pause until you do. The audience won't hold an initial pause against you, but if you start talking without having the main point in your mind, you may wander around the subject, convincing the audience you are disorganized.

The other steps are done as time permits. You can afford to start talking as soon as you have the main point. Simply state that point as your opening and proceed. So long as you keep the main point in mind, whatever you say on the subject will tend to support it. If you get to the end without having thought of a clever closing, simply summarize what you have said and restate your main point.

Impromptu Outlines

If you are in a situation with slightly more time, you could scribble an outline:

STATUS OF THE PROJECT
1. Good news/bad news
2. Behind -- Need help
   Last = 60% more
   Tried borrowing
   Tried temporaries
   Was 10 days – now 3 weeks
3. Good news/bad news

Sample Impromptu

Can you really come up with a professional quality speech in just a few seconds or minutes? If you focus your mind properly, you definitely can. A few years go I taught the Four-Step Impromptu Technique to a group of Air Force engineers as part of a briefing workshop. Then, each of them gave an impromptu speech. I asked one man to talk on ''My Role in My Organization's Mission.'' Here is how he began:

> *Imagine you are flying an Air Force aircraft. Everything is going fine until you hear a noise and look out the cockpit window. The left wingtip starts to vibrate and then breaks off. That throws the plane into a spin. You can't stop the spin, so you punch out in the ejection seat. Doing that, you save your own life, but the Air Force loses a ten million dollar aircraft. If those of us in the Structural Fractures Analysis Branch had been doing our job, that sort of accident would not happen.*

He explained the mission of the Structural Fractures Analysis Branch – inspecting and testing cracks in airframes and components to determine if the part in question would fail under stress. He explained his role as an inspector, including the sorts of test procedures he had available. To close, he said:

> *Now that you have heard what we do in the Structural Fractures Analysis Branch, you should feel safer the next time you ride in an Air Force aircraft.*

Whether you have twenty seconds or twenty minutes to prepare, you can manage to give a coherent speech if you keep your priorities in mind. No one expects you to improvise the Gettysburg Address, but if you can deliver a simple, but organized, presentation of your thoughts, your listeners will be amazed at your powers.

Executive Summary

1. When you must speak without having adequate preparation time, use the Four-Step Approach:

   A. Main Point

   B. Support

   C. Opening

   D. Closing

2. Do not start talking before you have a main point.

3. By keeping your mind focused on the main point, you can afford to start talking before you decide on the last three steps.

19

The Sales Presentation

A sales presentation is a special kind of speech, similar to other speeches, but different in some ways. A book the size of this one cannot tell you in one chapter all you might ever need to know about marketing and salesmanship. If you are in sales full-time, you should go to the library and check the dozens of books available on the subject.

If you are not selling full-time, this chapter will be useful. As a manager, you are likely to get roped into a *de facto* sales presentation eventually.

Perhaps you have expertise with a particular part of your organization's work and the prospect wants to talk to "somebody who knows this product inside and out."

Perhaps you have become known as a good speaker and your organization needs someone to beef up its briefing team for a major proposal.

Your responsibilities may be enlarged so the people who secure government grants or service major corporate clients report to you. You need to understand sales presentations to see if your team can do it better.

Often you will find yourself involved in internal sales, trying to sell a new method, a new project, or your department's product to others within your organization.

For whatever reason, you may find yourself having to sell something with a speech. That's what this chapter is all about.

The Motivated Sequence

In the chapter on Organizing to Persuade, we discussed the Motivated Sequence (The Madison Avenue Pattern) as a framework for organizing a speech. The basic sequence had five steps:

Arouse

Dissatisfy

Gratify

Picture

Move

Depending on your audience analysis, you may not need to do all of these steps in the speech itself. No matter what product or service you are trying to sell, what you are actually doing is offering to satisfy some need the prospect feels. The first step, then, either before or during the presentation, is to find out what needs the prospect is feeling. If the prospect is keenly aware of a problem which your product can solve, you can skip the first two steps on the Motivated Sequence. The audience is already aroused and dissatisfied. If you aren't sure of the prospect's needs, ask about challenges the organization is facing and listen carefully.

The Interactive Approach

The traditional sales presentation, in which the seller makes a highly polished speech in praise of the product, is overrated. A better format, in most cases, is the interactive approach, which draws responses from the audience. In effect, the audience steers the speech; by stating their objections, concerns, and favorite features, they guide the speaker to the presentation modules which will be most effective. By staying audience-centered, the speaker is likely to be less polished, but more convincing.

Ed Oakley has developed the question format into an art form; he gets people to convince themselves. Whether he is talking to a single decision-maker or a group, he asks what successes they have had recently. Doing so *arouses* their interest; everyone takes pleasure in describing victories. Also, by reviewing problems that have been solved, the audience convinces itself that the current crop of problems is likewise manageable. Ed asks what challenges the organization is facing, and by their answers the audience members persuade themselves they are dissatisfied with the status quo.

He explains how his program can help them meet those challenges (*gratify*) and asks them to describe the end result they want (*picture*). Finally, he summarizes what has been said and invites them to sign a contract (*move*).

Seeing it described this way, you may be thinking this approach doesn't involve presentations. It is more like a structured conversation. The interactive approach can be just a conversation with the decision-maker across a desk, but it can also be a full-blown, stand-up presentation with professional graphics and working models. Either way, the presentation needs to be constructed and practiced as stand-alone modules. If a briefing team will be doing the presentation, different people may take different subjects.

Suppose the prospect answers the question about challenges by explaining how worried the group is about having a guaranteed supply of raw materials. They have only limited stockpiles, and if the raw material supply line is interrupted, even briefly, they face a costly shutdown. The briefing team chief responds by asking another team member (the Director of Purchasing) to explain how they guarantee a steady flow of raw materials. The Director of Purchasing then shifts into a rehearsed module, explaining how the department has negotiated firm, long-term contracts with raw material producers. By lengthening the term of the typical contract, they have locked in a steady flow of materials. If the prospect is worried about cash flow, the team chief turns to the team's financial expert, who gives the presentation module on payment options.

Expect Resistance

Even if you have the obvious answer to a need the prospect is keenly aware of, you may encounter stiff resistance. Why? Because of inertia.

Whatever you are selling, no matter how good it is, represents change. A financial analyst may be struggling with an antiquated manual accounts system posted by high school dropouts who can't copy two numbers without making a mistake. You offer her a completely automated system in which every entry only has to be made once. After that, there is no chance for a copying error. The workload will drop so much she can fire the three dropouts and retain her one competent assistant. But she raises objections at every turn in your presentation.

Although the analyst knows the present system is a nightmare, it is at least a familiar nightmare. No matter how good your system is, she suspects it will bring its own problems, for which she is unprepared. Plus, there are substantial costs and risks involved in addition to the money. Her department is chronically behind, and she will have to shut down for a time to start the new system. If something goes wrong, she will have to call for outside help, exposing her dirty linen to the world. The present system is awful, but she inherited it, so no one holds it against her. If she approves the new system and it doesn't work, her boss will blame her for poor judgment.

So she raises objections. You need to realize this is not a true adversary relationship. The prospect is not trying to shoot down the sale. She is asking you to reassure her that her worst fears are invalid. If you have a valuable (and costly) product, you should expect prospects to be reluctant, to say *no* several times before they say *yes*. You may even find people who raise phony objections just to draw out the proceedings so they won't appear to be making snap judgments. The whole team working on a sales presentation should understand that every objection provides an opening for a sale. Prospects rarely object out of idle curiosity – objections normally mean people are ready to buy if their apprehension can be reduced.

You should anticipate likely objections (just as you anticipate likely questions after other speeches) and have appropriate responses ready. In your rehearsals, you should practice fielding objections and closing the sale after the objections are met.

Expect Nervousness

With other types of speeches you are normally nervous while the audience is calm. In a sales presentation, the audience may be as nervous as you are. Consider a Department of Defense committee evaluating new aircraft designs from competing companies. A significant mistake in judgment could impact the career of every committee member. Other audiences may have less money at stake, but they will typically feel the pressure of having to make important decisions while in the spotlight.

Because they are nervous, you need to be calm and take special pains to make them feel at ease. Chat with the prospects before your speech begins; in your introduction, stress things you have in common; and add a judicious touch of humor. If you appear relaxed, they are likely to relax as well.

Analyze the Audience

You would want to do this anyway, of course. But in a sales presentation, knowing who the decision-maker is becomes doubly important. Which of those people in front of you can approve the sale? You may be able to find out in advance, but if you can't, study the interactions of the audience. Do members of the other firm seem to be taking their cues from one person? If so, you should pay extra close attention to that person's comments and questions.

If the decision-maker does something which suggests a negative reaction to something you said, stop and ask a question. ("You seem a little puzzled. Do you have any concerns over what I just said?") Try to draw out negative feelings so you can deal with them and relieve the prospect's anxiety. Sometimes the decision-maker's body language will be ambiguous. Without speculating on what you saw, you can still provide an opening. ("Does anyone have a question at this point?")

Close the Deal

Every speech is an attempt at persuasion. A sales presentation is simply a more overt attempt. In the conclusion to your speech, you need to state clearly what action you want the prospect to take. You want to make a sale, obviously, but what do you want the prospect to do today? Whatever you want should be stated explicitly.

Although the presentation is planned with a call for action at the end, no divine law requires you to give the whole presentation. If in answering an objection in the middle of the speech, you sense the prospect is ready to buy, cut to the end and ask for the sale. Giving the rest of the presentation allows the prospect time to re-evaluate the decision and back out. Professional sales people summarize this concept with a bit of jargon: *Don't talk past the close!*

Most decision-makers, however, will hear the whole presentation before deciding. After ending your presentation with a call for action, you should be prepared to wait. Big decisions are not made instantly. If no action seems to be forthcoming, it would be appropriate to raise another question (or comment) to nudge the prospect toward a decision. ("Would you like the renovation to start on Tuesday or the following week?" or "If you want to sign the purchase order now, I wouldn't have to interrupt by coming back later.")

After you have made that slight push, just wait. Let the silence weigh on the prospect. You have put together the best possible presentation and now the ball is in the other court.

Executive Summary

1. The most effective sales presentations are interactive.

2. Ask questions to lead the audience through the Motivated Sequence (Arouse - Dissatisfy - Gratify - Picture - Move).

3. Expect resistance from serious prospects.

4. An objection indicates serious interest. Answer the objection and close the sale.

5. Watch the audience to determine who is the real decision-maker.

20

The After-Dinner Speech

While giving a presentation in your line of work is a necessity, giving an after-dinner speech is a form of indulgence – and everyone needs to be indulged once in a while. The featured speaker at a dinner meeting becomes an honored guest, the center of attention. You may want to become a regular speaker on the dinner circuit in your town, or a professional speaker specializing in after-dinner events, or you may want to speak only at occasional special events. In any event, be prepared for at least a mild ego trip.

After-dinner speeches can be informative, entertaining, or ceremonial – or they can be a mixture. They may also be overtly persuasive, provided the persuasion is not heavy handed.

Informative

Anyone who has heard more than a few after-dinner speeches from more than one organization realizes how broad the range of subjects is. In fact, when you become known as an accomplished speaker, groups will sometimes ask you to speak on any subject you choose. Even if a group asks you to talk on a particular theme, they will often be open to compromise.

Given that openness about possible topics, your best bet is to work up several enlightening speeches on subjects that interest you and give them over and over with appropriate modifications. Some people can give the same speech for thirty years and make it sound fresh every time, but if you find one of yours going stale, you should consider replacing it.

What should you talk about? Strange as it seems, the general public will probably find certain aspects of your job fascinating. I have heard speakers hold an audience in thrall with such seemingly stupefying topics as "How Neurons Work" and "How Does a Novelist Ever Get Published." A good place to start when looking for a good work-related topic is your own store of anecdotes. When you start swapping stories with friends, what do you tell them about your work place? Chances are, the best of those stories contain the kernel of a good speech.

In fact, anecdotes also provide you one of the richest sources of supporting material. Dinner audiences (or luncheon audiences, for that matter) generally do not want to hear a lawyer discuss the constitutional underpinnings of the Miranda Doctrine. They want to hear him talk about the clients, judges, and attorneys he has known and the strange things he has seen them do. People are curious. They want to vicariously experience the more interesting parts of your life at work.

Hobbies are another abundant source for informative speeches. The freedom you have in choosing a topic should let you focus on the one thing you do that fascinates you the most. My friend, John Stibravy, who holds a Ph.D. in English, spends most of his spare time getting grease on his hands and soot on his face while running old, cantankerous steam engines. When he gives a talk with slides of belching engines and tales of crusty engineers, people love it – because he loves it.

Not that people are afraid to think after dinner. You can talk about the problems or challenges facing society; those are interesting, too – if you talk about them from a human perspective.

Entertaining After Dinner

Almost every speech can benefit from a judicious infusion of humor, but some after-dinner speeches have little else. The goal of the speech is to keep people laughing. You can give a humorous speech on just about any occasion you would give an informative speech, but the risks are higher. If you sense the audience is uninterested in part of your informative speech, you can skip parts of that section and move on to the next part. But if you are giving an entertaining speech and the jokes start to bomb, you may lose the audience before you can recover.

On the other hand, giving a speech is like betting on the horses: the higher the risk, the higher the gain. Genuinely funny speakers achieve a fame beyond those who merely inform. Mark Twain and Will Rogers are still renowned more than 75 and 50 years after their last speeches.

In his book, *Communicating at the Top*[23], George de Mare lists categories of humor appropriate to speeches. The list is worth reviewing now and then when you are searching for a workable idea.

Anticlimax: A sudden deliberate letdown.

> *In our country, we have three unspeakably precious things: freedom of speech, freedom of conscience, and the prudence not to practice either.*
> Mark Twain

Understatement: Also startling.

> *A funny thing happened to me on the way to the White House.*
> Adlai Stevenson

Use of Others Famed Witticisms: Look through an anthology for appropriate quotes (always giving proper credit to the author).

> *Farming looks mighty easy when your plow is a pencil, and you're a thousand miles from a corn field.*
> Dwight Eisenhower

Incongruity: Building up a logical or grammatical context and then slipping in an out-of-place idea.

> *An Englishman thinks seated; a Frenchman standing; an American pacing; an Irishman afterwards.*
> Austin O'Malley

Exaggeration: Simply overstating something is not enough. Saying, "I got a million phone calls today," won't draw a laugh (maybe not even a smile). To be funny, exaggeration must be somehow outrageous or clever.

> *American women expect to find in their husbands a perfection that English women only hope to find in their butlers.*
> Somerset Maugham

Humorous Definitions and Comparisons:

> *Bore: A person who talks when you wish him to listen.*
>
> Ambrose Bierce

Plays on Words: Use with caution. What is funny to you may be a groaner to the audience.

> *Anti-Nudity Law To Get Closer Look*
>
> Newspaper headline[24]

Self-Deprecation:

> *If I had two faces, I wouldn't wear this one.*
>
> Abraham Lincoln

Humorous Self-Flattery:

> *In those days he was wiser than he is now; he used frequently to take my advice.*
>
> Winston Churchill

Topical References: A quick-witted speaker can sometimes convert recent news material or comments made by other people on the occasion into funny material. Several years ago my dad was asked to speak at an organization's Christmas party. Early in the program, the moderator explained the agenda and mentioned that ''after Ross speaks we will have some fun'' (with Christmas carols, Santa Claus, etc.) When Dad got up to speak he apologized (tongue in cheek) for being a wet blanket and promised to hold his speech short, so as not to delay the fun.

I would add **Tongue-in-Cheek Logic** to de Mare's list. Several years ago I worked up a speech on creativity and gave it to a number of groups. A central illustration in the speech was an improved mousetrap invented by a very creative man named A. C. Hansen. I began the speech with this bit of wacky logic:

> *Have you ever thought what we are doing to the I.Q. of the mouse population in this country? Consider this – when you get a mouse in your house, what's the first thing you do? If you are like the average American, you go down to the store*

and buy one of these conventional mousetraps. [I hold one up.] You take it home, bait it, set it, and then go to bed.

When you check in the morning, one of three things has happened. Either the mouse took the night off, and the trap is undisturbed. Or a smart mouse came along, tripped the trap, and ate the bait. (The smart mice get us trained. We feed them every night on this wooden platter [hold up wooden mouse-trap], so they don't have to forage any more.)

The other possibility – a dumb mouse came along and got nailed in the trap. Now you've got a dead mouse to dispose of.

This illustrates the problem. The dumb mice keep getting cut off in the prime of life; the smart mice get to live and reproduce. By the laws of genetics, each generation of mice is smarter than the one before. This type of trap has only been around for 150 years and already the mice have figured it out. If this process goes undisturbed for another thousand years, our descendants will be contending with a PLAGUE OF GENIUS MICE!

Whatever material you use, remember that entertaining speeches have structure, just as other speeches do. You still need a beginning, middle, and ending, as well as a thread that ties everything together.

Ceremonial

By now, you have probably realized that not all after-dinner type speeches are given after dinner. A retirement ceremony could be scheduled at almost any time in the day or evening, but the required speech more closely resembles an after-dinner speech than the presentation you might give to senior staff members on impending budget constraints.

Ceremonial occasions come in all shapes and colors: retirements, Hale and Farewell events, anniversaries of important milestones, openings of new branches, installations of officers, celebrations of particular awards or victories, and many more. Social gatherings which do not mark any particular achievement or occasion are also likely to have a definite ceremonial aspect. Because ceremonies play an important role in bonding people together, managers cannot afford to slight them, even if they are inconvenient.

Planning a ceremonial speech is like planning any other speech, except that the occasion is a more important factor than usual. The mood of the occasion should govern the tone of your speech. Is this to be a raucous victory dinner or a quiet gathering of friends who want to express their appreciation to one of their number who is leaving after 40 years? No matter how well-planned and well-rehearsed the speech, it will be ineffective if the tone is not appropriate.

Two of the most useful components of a ceremonial speech are sincerity and appropriate humor. Obvious flattery can make a ceremonial speech seem cheap. Calling a retiring supervisor "One of the historic leaders of our industry," will create embarrassment rather than honoring the person. It is better to be sincere and talk about what he or she has actually done.

The subject of a retirement speech is obvious; other ceremonies may lack that tight focus. What can we say to honor Arbor Day or National Wool-Growers Month? When you are asked to speak on a ceremonial occasion and must find your own topic, consider the acronym HOP.

H = History

O = Organization

P = Purpose

History: Look for stories to build a presentation around. What does this day commemorate? What memorable characters are associated with it? What did they do? What do you remember doing on previous celebrations like this one. ("On Veterans Day, years ago, I remember standing with my dad, with our hats off, reverently watching the changing of the guard at the Tomb of the Unknown Soldier.")

Organization: What stories can you find about the group that is sponsoring you? How does that group connect with the celebration? What can you say about heroes in the organization's past? The human interest stories you are looking for do not have to be heavy. Once, in speaking to a Kiwanis Club, I recalled an incredibly expensive double-date with my college roommate. We took two girls we barely knew to dinner and a movie. What I remember from the dinner was a momentary financial crisis when we got the check – it was over $16. The movie, I remember, was *Lilies of the Field*, starring Sidney Portier. A group of German nuns was trying to build a chapel in a desert location in the American Southwest with a lot of assistance from God and Sidney Portier. At one point, the mother superior was counting the checks donated by local service clubs:

Und here is from Elks, und here is from Lions, und here is from Kiwanis – WHAT KIND OF ANIMAL IS KIWANIS?!

Purpose: Look at the specific purpose of the celebration and the broader purpose behind it. Arbor Day is about more than tree planting; you can talk about our role in managing the earth's environment. Veterans Day is about more than courage in the face of enemy fire; the sacrifice of those veterans calls us to redouble our efforts to build a lasting structure of peace.

Humor: Ceremonies exist to bind people together, and humor is one of the better means to this end. Look for ways to work in humor to get people in the proper mood for the occasion. Anecdotes work well in this kind of speech. If you are celebrating Gloria's promotion, tell about the time she had to crawl in the heating duct to get her key. If you are speaking on the 125th anniversary of your *alma mater*, tell how the founder saved the college from bankruptcy by hiding the financial records in his barn. Many ceremonial speeches are nothing but a string of anecdotes wound around a central theme.

Whether after dinner, after lunch, or after the coffee break, a good after-dinner speech will leave the audience in the right frame of mind.

Executive Summary

1. After-dinner speakers usually have a broad choice of topics. Pick something that fascinates you. For possibilities, look at the subjects of the anecdotes you like to tell.

2. To get ideas for humor, glance through the humor categories in this chapter.

3. Speeches on ceremonial occasions must be suitable for the mood of the occasion.

4. For speech ideas on a ceremonial occasion, work with the acronym HOP (History - Organization - Purpose).

21

Teaching

Teaching seems to be a hidden responsibility in many management jobs. Teaching may never be mentioned in an MBA program and it may not show up on a job description, but many managers see no way to avoid it. The reasons are not hard to see. Let's assume you are an expert at some skill which is in short supply. The skill could be anything: writing proposals, managing subordinates, scheduling production, identifying new clients – anything. Assuming you are known to be an articulate speaker, it is only a matter of time before someone asks you to teach a course in order to share what you know.

As a manager, you also must arrange training for inexperienced employees. Some managers are very lucky; they simply turn the task over to the training department. Most of us are not so lucky. We end up arranging all the training for subordinates and doing much of it personally.

Evaluating the Requirement

Giving a teaching lecture is not especially difficult (despite the fact many lectures are terrible). The difficult part is deciding when you actually need to lecture. Sometimes people are asked to teach subjects that should not be taught, and sometimes teachers choose to lecture when another method would be superior.

Before you get very far into planning a lecture, you need to look at alternatives. Some organizations seem to take for granted that any deficient performance indicates a need for training. In fact, most of the time, training should be considered as the last alternative. Considering the time and pay scales of teacher and students, training is usually quite expensive. Take a look at other ways to improve performance without formal training.[25]

Improve the tools. If your sales reps keep fouling up an order form, you can train the reps, and later train their replacements, and their replacements . . . Or you can simplify the form.

Remove obstacles. If managers never seem to get their quarterly budget updates in on time, they may need more training on the budget process, or they may need help with an obstacle. (Perhaps the computer is always tied up at the end of the quarter.)

Fire and hire. Every task takes some innate ability. Realistically, some people lack the potential for a particular job.

Arrange practice. What if your proposal briefing team only pitches one proposal a year and usually blows it. Do they need more training or just more dry runs?

Provide feedback. If the experienced people in your graphics shop are doing sloppy work, you can train them again – or you can ship every mistake back to them for correction. Too often, organizations pour training on a problem when the people causing the problem are honestly unaware anything is wrong.

Rearrange incentives. The carrot-and-stick approach can be very effective – unless you have the carrot at the back end of the horse.

Choosing the Training Method

Suppose you have examined the other choices and training seems to be the most cost-effective alternative. Now you must decide how to train. Consider what you want the employee to be able to do. If the task involves a complicated process (such as giving a speech) the training should involve some form of practice or simulation (as in a speech workshop). If the students need to learn background information, but the information is written down in a clear form, just let the students read it and then question or test them about it. Most teachers lecture for no reason except that they were taught by teachers who lectured.

So, when should you lecture? Only when the material is fairly simple and requires emphasis or interaction with the students.

Lecturing

Let's suppose you have been roped into teaching a class. You have examined the situation and agreed there is no real alternative to training. After looking at other methods, you choose lecturing as the most effective method. You design a two-day course with each day having five hours of lecture, one hour of discussion, and one hour of role playing. Then reality hits! The last time you gave a twenty minute speech, you spent hours preparing and rehearsing it. Without quitting your regular job, how can you possibly get ready for ten hours of lecturing?

You have just encountered one of the fundamental differences between classroom lectures and other speeches. The ratio of preparation time to delivery time is radically different. (Unless, of course, you teach the same material over and over or you teach only a brief segment now and then.)

Most teachers in this situation adjust by dropping most of the rehearsals. They prepare an outline (usually on paper rather than cards, due to the volume of information) and improvise from it. Throughout your school years, you saw dozens of teachers use this technique. Not all of them used it well; I caution you to think through what you are doing rather than simply imitating what you have seen.

Some of the things that can go wrong in a lecture should be obvious to you because they can go wrong in any speech. But you may encounter other more subtle problems generated by the nature of the situation.

Modeling: Remember, students will retain far more factual information if they read it than if they hear it. The purpose of a lecture is to make the material more vivid or to increase the interaction between the instructor and the students. For that reason, your role as a model for the students becomes critically important. In a lecture, the effect you have on students' attitudes toward the subject is likely to be more important than what you say about the subject.

Let's go back to the hypothetical situation. You plan to teach a two-day class with ten lecture hours and four other classroom hours. In two days you will spend more face-to-face time with those students than their spouses do in five days. If you show by your actions that the subject is important and interesting, most of them will come to regard it in the same light. Research has demonstrated conclusively what has always been intuitively obvious: students who are attracted to a subject study more and concentrate harder than those who try to avoid the subject. Since these effects continue after the class is over, the results are compounded.

Classroom Behavior

Everything you do in the classroom should reinforce the idea that you are interested in the students and in the subject. Do not let the fact you had poor or mediocre teachers as models trap you into doing things that are counter-productive. Instead of blindly following what you have seen other teachers do, consider the options. Each of the following suggestions has solid evidence from classroom research behind it. Many of these ideas seem too self-evident to mention, except for the fact I have seen managers violating them.[26]

You should not ...

Sit behind a desk while lecturing. It puts a barrier between you and the class. Sitting on a desk or on a chair in the open is slightly better. Standing is recommended.

Stand behind a lectern. Instead, put your notes on the lectern and stand to the side.

Make negative comments about students or their work, especially in front of the class.

Ask questions expecting a canned answer.

Belittle students for their comments or answers to questions. You should reward those who participate, not just those with the right answer. Rewarding *rightness* and criticizing *wrongness* will discourage everyone, since no one is always right. The quickest reward is a positive comment.

Start late. Doing so punishes those who came on time.

You should ...

Come early and chat with the students.

Start on time.

Talk about your own experiences. (But don't lose track of the lesson plan.)

Encourage students to talk.

Respond to *every* student comment. You can't afford to ignore even off-the-wall comments. If you can't think of a better response, say, ''That is an interesting opinion.''

Include humor.

Learn students' names quickly and use them often.

Talk to students when you run into them elsewhere.

Ask for student input on assignment requirements, due dates, and topics.

Ask open-ended questions. Praise student work, comments, and actions.

Be animated in movement and gestures.

Keep eye contact.

Smile.

Be relaxed in posture.

Move around the room while talking.

Have an energetic vocal delivery.

Teaching, like after-dinner speaking, can be enjoyable, because the types of behavior that make it successful are the things most people enjoy doing anyway.

Executive Summary

1. Teaching is a hidden responsibility in many management jobs.

2. Force of habit causes people to lecture when other methods would be more effective.

3. Always consider alternatives to training first.

4. If training is necessary, consider alternatives to lecturing.

5. Lecture only when the material is fairly simple and requires interaction or emphasis.

6. The attitude you model while lecturing is likely to be more important than what you say.

7. Practice open classroom behavior.

22

Introducing Another Speaker

You've all got the speaker's biography in your info packet, so, instead of me introducing her, you can just read it for yourself.

Our speaker's gonna talk about "Closing the Sale," which reminds me of the traveling salesman that got caught in a storm . . .

Today's speaker was born at 6:37 A.M in the tiny hamlet of Hutto, Texas. She was the third of four children, one of whom died in infancy. She attended Nellie Rose Elementary School for eight years, during which she learned to play a musical instrument . . .

We couldn't get the speaker we really wanted, so we got this guy to fill in for us.

Judging from the number of bad introductions like those above, the art of introducing a speaker appears to be a closely kept secret. This is unfortunate since a good introduction motivates the audience to listen, gets their minds on the right wavelength (subject), and raises their expectations of the speaker. A good introducer pulls the audience up to speed and then hands them to the speaker with no loss of momentum.

Organizing the Introduction

Introducing a speaker will be less stressful if you call ahead of time to collect information. Waiting until just before the speech to ask the speaker can be risky; both the speaker and introducer may be occupied with other concerns. At the time of the initial call, some speakers try to send a bio sketch or resume for the introducer to dig through for introductory material. I have found it easier to get the information for the introduction by asking the speaker direct questions.

Collecting the information and structuring the introduction will both be easier if you remember the acronym SIS.

S = Subject

I = Importance

S = Speaker

Subject: The audience needs to know the title of the speech and the subject if the title does not make it clear. For an audience unfamiliar with the subject, the introducer may give part of the background information, unless the speaker prefers to do it.

Importance: How does the subject concern this audience? Why should they listen? What can they gain from this speaker?

Speaker: What connects this speaker to this audience? What do they have in common? What experience does the speaker have with the subject? What credentials allow the speaker to speak as an authority?

Staying in Balance: As an introducer, you should remember your job is to launch the speaker under favorable conditions; you should not give the speech! To keep the introduction in proper perspective to the rest of the speech, its length should be no more than ten percent of the length of the speech. You will recall that the first part of the speech itself, what Aristotle called the *beginning*, is also referred to as an *introduction.* To keep the speech in balance, that introductory part of the speech should be no more than ten to twenty percent of the total. Whenever a separate person introduces the speaker, their two introductions need to complement each other. For instance, when the introducer covers the speaker's credentials, the speaker does not need to. If the introducer has a fairly long introduction (ten percent), the speaker will be able to scale back his introduction to ten percent.

Sticking to the Subject: Introducers frequently add irrelevant material. Resist the temptation. An audience normally does not care when or where a speaker was born. Exceptions – if the speech is on geriatrics or social security, the speaker's age may be important; if the speaker's birthplace is near the site of the speech, saying so may aid in building rapport. Details about the speaker's spouse or children are irrelevant, unless the speech is about parenting. The audience wants to know how the speaker's life connects with them and the subject. Other information just clouds the picture.

Delivering the Introduction

Many experienced speakers have been burned by bad introductions; therefore, some speakers will try to pressure you into reading word-for-word an introduction they have written. If the speaker understands the SIS requirement, the introduction will probably be well designed, but reading an introduction has the same drawbacks as reading a speech.

I suggest you highlight the key phrases in the typed copy the speaker gives you, so you can use that typed page as an outline. If the speaker is still uneasy, give a demonstration. Say, "Here's what I plan to say." Then give the introduction as you would to the audience. Once the speaker realizes you are a competent speaker who will stick to the pertinent information instead of dragging in a bunch of corny stories, he should relent.

If, despite your best efforts, you are forced to read the introduction, rehearse by reading it aloud several times, marking pauses and words to emphasize.

When You are the Speaker

Anytime you do not know the introducer, there is a possibility you will get a disorganized, inarticulate introduction. You can lessen that possibility by creating your own introduction using the SIS model. Prepare a word-for-word script (in case the introducer is inexperienced) and a key-word outline (in case the speaker is experienced). Send copies of the outline and script in advance, so the introducer will have time to study them. Bring additional copies on the day of the speech in case the introducer forgets hers. When you consult with the introducer, let her know it is important for her to cover each of the ideas in the outline. Otherwise, the audience may miss vital information.

Executive Summary

1. Sound introductions are built on the acronym SIS (Subject - Importance - Speaker).

2. When you find you will be introducing someone, call the speaker and collect the SIS information. At the same time, check whether the speaker wants you to cover some of the background on the subject.

3. When you are the speaker, compose a word-for-word introduction and a key-word outline of the introduction; send both to the introducer and take additional copies with you when you go to speak.

23

Speaking Professionally

If you enjoy speaking and are good at it, you may have wondered what it would take to become a professional. Exactly what it would take varies depending on what part of the business you are going into. For years, people who consider themselves professional speakers have attempted to define the *profession* of speaking without making very much headway. The field does not have sharp-edged boundaries like the medical profession.

Varieties of Professional Speaking

Some people who are excellent and give numerous speeches never get paid directly for a speech. They are management consultants, accountants, psychologists, divorce lawyers, decorators, and the like, who use speaking as a marketing tool to bring in clients.

In another group are speakers who charge their audiences nothing because they are sponsored by corporations or foundations. They speak free at conferences, conventions, and trade shows while collecting a salary or fees from the sponsor, who values the publicity.

Still another group charges the audience little or nothing for the speech, but uses each speech to generate massive book and tape sales from the back of the room.

Others who consider themselves speakers would be more accurately described as trainers or seminar leaders. Some of these promote themselves independently. Others contract with national seminar companies, such as CareerTrack, Fred Pryor, SkillPath, and Seminars International. These people travel the country putting on public seminars, as well as conducting training on site for different organizations.

The one group everyone agrees is in the speaking profession consists of people who get virtually all their income from clients who pay them for keynote and motivational speeches. As you would expect, each of these speaking groups can be further sub-divided.

Anyone considering a speaking career should attend as many speeches or seminars as possible to determine which particular part of the market fits their talents.

Speaking Income

Among the things professional speakers and actors have in common is the widespread perception that their incomes are huge and their lives constantly exciting. The reality for union actors in New York is an 80% unemployment rate and poverty-level incomes for many of those who work. The picture for professional speakers is not that bad, but neither is the profession a gold mine.

The casual observer who reads that Tom Peters and Henry Kissinger get over $40,000 for a single speech may conclude the public is wildly throwing money at anyone with enough nerve to stand on a stage behind a microphone.

In reality, only good celebrity speakers can get five-figure speaking fees. Professional speakers whose names are not household words can command fees of $3500 to $10,000 only if they are at the top of their field and have an ongoing, highly effective marketing campaign. That segment of the market is extremely competitive, meaning speakers at the top must keep marketing just to hold their positions. The marketing may be done by the speaker, whose available time is limited by frequent travel, by the speaker's paid staff, or by speakers bureaus.

Speaker's bureaus function as brokers between speakers and trainers and the people who hire them. A typical bureau will charge a speaker a commission of about 20% to 35% plus a retainer or marketing fee up front. Some bureaus engage in broad-based advertising and direct marketing; all of them use direct contact to close sales with meeting planners, association executives, and human resource directors.

Many speakers use all three avenues (themselves, their staffs, and bureaus) for marketing.

The market segment with fees between $500 and $3500 is broad and varied. Some established speakers and trainers in this bracket could push their fees much higher, but they enjoy speaking more than marketing. By undercutting the top bracket in price, they stay booked without a massive marketing effort. Speakers for whom this strategy is working may function without a staff, depending on bureaus to set up most of their engagements.

Other speakers and trainers in this price range are working in market niches where no one gets a high fee. The soundness of this strategy can be illustrated by the fact there are more successful Chevrolet dealers than Mercedes dealers.

Another group of speakers is working its way up to the top bracket by repeated fee increases and a steadily expanding marketing effort.

Speakers whose regular fees are below $500 may have difficulty staying credible as full-time speakers. I have heard of fees as low as $50, but organizations paying $50-$500 generally expect to get an accomplished part-timer.

National seminar companies (of which only a handful are named above) are an exception to this $500 threshold. Their trainers may work for $400/day plus expenses, but they get a commission on back-of-room sales, and they get a lot of work.

Assessing the Prospects

In my years as a professional trainer and speaker, I have seen a number of talented, hard-working people fail to establish themselves full-time in the profession. Each of them seemed to lack one or more of these essential elements:

1. Subject matter expertise. Audiences want more than entertainment. They want increased knowledge and skills.

2. A clearly defined market niche.

3. A sense of mission. A conviction that what you are doing will make the world better. People enter my speaking workshops feeling trapped; they know they can't advance professionally without better speaking skills, and they doubt their own ability. The workshop does more than make them better speakers. By getting over that hurdle, they feel they are in control of

their destiny again. Knowing that workshop changes people's lives makes my marketing convincing.

4. A sense of fun. If you do not enjoy what you are doing, neither will the audience. If they don't enjoy it, you won't be invited back.

5. A sound business plan.

6. A sound marketing plan and the patience to follow it. Changing targets every week is a formula for disaster.

7. Sufficient energy. If people can't hear excitement in your voice, they wonder how you can keep an audience awake.

8. Sufficient determination. Some of the most successful professional speakers are single mothers. With no other salary to depend on, they do whatever it takes to make this career work.

9. Enough speaking experience to handle the unexpected.

10. Sufficient financial reserves. A speaking business is like any other business – it will not be instantly successful. Some people who hire speakers and trainers have a long buying cycle, but even those who don't have a touch of the herd instinct. They want to see you have been around for awhile before they risk hiring you. Realistically, you should be able to support your family for two years before the business becomes consistently profitable.

Getting From Here to There

For most people, the best way to get from another job to a professional speaking career is to build the speaking business part-time until it occupies every free moment. When the requests for paid speaking engagements outnumber the available speaking dates, it is time to go full-time.

At the same time the speaker is picking up engagements, he or she should be developing business and marketing plans and making contacts throughout the speaking profession. Anyone having trouble developing a business plan or marketing plan should call the nearest large chamber of commerce and ask for the Small Business Development Council. Their guidance can be invaluable.

For learning the ropes in the profession, the best strategy is to become active in professional associations. Anyone who is serious about full-time speaking or training needs to be a member of at least two associations: one representing the speaking profession and one connected with the selected market niche. The first association lets you rub shoulders with other speakers and trainers, which can accelerate your learning curve and keep you from reinventing the wheel. The second association connects you with people who are in the market for your services; by learning their needs, you learn how to improve your services and marketing.

The most well-rounded association in the speaking profession is the National Speakers Association (NSA), which is listed in the Resource List (pp. 261-264). NSA, which also accepts international members, has active chapters in many parts of the U.S. Through a number of programs, NSA helps its members learn to run speaking businesses. It also helps people who are already professional caliber speakers and trainers refine their skills, and provides opportunities for members to showcase their talents. A number of successful collaborative ventures owe their genesis to networking at NSA functions.

Anyone involved in training should also check out the American Society for Training and Development (ASTD). ASTD has over 160 chapters throughout the U.S. A typical ASTD convention will have large numbers of corporate and government training directors; staff trainers (in-house); independent trainers; representatives of training firms; vendors of equipment, special supplies, and services; students; and job-seekers. With that sort of mixture, the probability of fruitful contacts is high.

The same techniques and media used in selling other high quality goods and services will work with speeches and seminars, but speakers and trainers have a couple of additional avenues not available to a seller of security services, for instance. Anyone who sells training should get listed with the various training information services in the Resource List. Each of these firms acts as a clearinghouse for training information. For a fee, a director of human resources can search the firm's database for trainers offering a particular subject. Any *bona fide* trainer can be listed in the database free of charge.

The other unique type of resource is the speakers bureau. The NSA directory has over 60 members listed under the category Speakers Bureau/ Service Organization. Walters Speaker Services publishes a directory which describes 415 bureaus in 12 countries. After you have enough experience to compete confidently in your market niche, you should begin contacting bureaus which handle your kind of work. The better ones will want to see you speak, either in person or on tape, before signing a contract.

A chapter on breaking into the professional ranks would not be complete without mentioning Dottie Walters. Her company, Walters Speaker Services, operates as a speakers bureau, but she also provides a number of valuable resources for speakers. In addition to seminars for professional speakers and the bureau directory mentioned above, she publishes a speakers newsmagazine, *Sharing Ideas*, and has authored the book, *Speak and Grow Rich*, both widely respected in the speaking profession.

Executive Summary

1. Professional speakers who are not celebrities can command fees of $3500 to $10,000 only if they are at the top of their field and have an ongoing, highly effective marketing campaign.

2. Speakers whose fees range from $500 to $3500 may be top-quality speakers who undercut the top price bracket to simplify their marketing. Others in this price range work in market niches where no one gets a top fee. Still others in this bracket are working their way to the top.

3. Many professional speakers rely heavily on speakers bureaus, which market them to prospective clients in return for a commission.

4. For most people, the best way to get from another job to a professional speaking career is to build the speaking business part-time until it occupies every free moment. Then make the jump.

24

Conclusion

In Chapter 2, I mentioned that all speeches are persuasive speeches. When I was a teenager, I once gave a speech where everything I tried worked. It was as if the audience of a thousand people was bound by a magic spell; wherever I led, they would follow. I had never imagined that anyone could possess the power I felt at that moment. I would like to say that every time I stand up to talk, the same thing happens – but it doesn't. I feel the same power briefly now and then.

In my mind, that feeling is linked to a similar sensation I had in the Air Force years later when I could reach out and put my hand on the controls of a nuclear weapon. No one in my position could fire a nuclear weapon; only the President had that power. It seemed incredible to me that one mortal could have so much control over the destiny of our planet. I prayed that God would give him wisdom.

This book tells you most of what I know about persuading people by speaking to them. But you should never forget the power of persuasion is the power to change people's lives. You can just as readily persuade people to join a bad cause as a good one. Because you know how to say things well, you must carefully choose what things you will say.

As your persuasive power increases, use it wisely.

Good luck and God speed!

Appendix I
Speech Reservation Form

Appendix I contains Master Copies of the Speech Reservation Form which can be copied and enlarged as often as necessary without the author's permission. To enlarge these sheets to $8^1/_2$" by 11", set your photocopier to enlarge 167%.

Speech Reservation Form

NOTE: When someone wants you to make a speech or presentation, use this form to record key information.

Organization: _____

Address: _____

_____

Contact: _____

Work phone: _____

Fax number: _____

Home phone: _____

Date of speech: _____

Location of speech: _____

Time speech begins: _____

Length of introduction: _____

Who will give the introduction? _____

Length of speech: _____

Length of question period: _____

Speech subject and title: _____

Speech purpose: _____

Speech Reservation Form   page 2

What particular aspects of the subject are you expected to cover? _____

_____

_____

Who else will speak? _____

What is the order of events/speeches? _____

Amount of fee or honorarium: _____

Amount for expenses: _____

How are expenses handled? _____

Amount paid in advance: _____

Will the organization furnish transportation from the airport? _____

Size of meeting room: _____

Number in audience: _____

Equipment furnished by sponsoring organization: _____

_____

_____

Equipment furnished by speaker: _____

_____

_____

Who else has spoken to this group recently?_____

_____

_____

Appendix II

Audience Analysis Worksheet

Appendix II contains Master Copies of the Audience Analysis Worksheet which can be copied and enlarged as often as necessary without the author's permission. To enlarge these sheets to 8½" by 11", set your photocopier to enlarge 167%.

Audience Analysis Worksheet

Speech date:_____ Speech purpose: _____

Sponsoring organization: _____

What you want to know about individuals:

1. Typical job positions and responsibilities: _____

2. Age range: youngest, oldest, average _____

3. Married or single? _____

4. Percentage of men to women: _____

5. Strong beliefs/taboos: _____

6. Why are they coming to hear you? _____

_____

7. What benefit do they expect from you? _____

8. Other expectations? _____

_____

9. Are they for or against your position? _____

10. Other things they may be worrying about: _____

_____

11. General education level: _____

Audience Analysis Worksheet   page 2

12. What they already know on the topic: ───────────────────────

13. What is their interest in the topic? ───────────────────────

14. Jargon and terms they use frequently: ──────────────────────

───

15. Any language difficulties? (English as a second language, etc.) ─────────

16. What values are important to them? ──────────────────────────

17. What constraints do they have? ────────────────────────────

18. What mood will you find them in? ──────────────────────────

19. What physical state will they be in? ────────────────────────

20. What has worked with this group in the past? ──────────────────

21. What are they likely to wear? ─────────────────────────────

What you want to know about the group

1. Organizational history: ─────────────────────────────────

2. Current challenges: ───────────────────────────────────

3. Organizational structure: ───────────────────────────────

4. Recent Successes: ────────────────────────────────────

5. Size: ──

6. Organizational mission or goals: ─────────────────────────

Audience Analysis Worksheet   page 3

7. Organizational self-image: _____

8. Recent disasters: _____

9. Is the organization growing or shrinking? _____

10. Key competitors: _____

11. Key people in the organization:

Name	Position	Role

12. Key people in the speech audience:

Name	Position	Role

Where to go for information

1. Your contact with the organization
2. Newspaper files
3. Standard reference works
4. Current employees or volunteers
5. Former employees or volunteers
6. Competitors
7. Previous speakers
8. Company annual report, brochures, and newsletters
9. Pre-speech questionnaire

Appendix III

ComSkills Speech Planner

Appendix III contains Master Copies of the *ComSkills* Speech Planner which can be copied and enlarged as often as necessary without the author's permission. To enlarge these sheets to $8^1/_2$" by 11", set your photocopier to enlarge 167%.

ComSkills Speech Planner

1. PURPOSE: What do you want the audience to do as a result of your speech? Be specific.

NOTE: Before proceeding, take a separate sheet of paper and brainstorm the speech, listing all the ideas you can think of that relate to this purpose.

2. KEY PLAYERS: Describe the principal decision-makers in the audience.

Name	Position	Decision-making Role

3. MOTIVATION: Why should audience members care about your topic? What will they gain by doing what you want?

4. MAJOR POINT: State *in one sentence* the most important idea you want the audience to remember.

ComSkills Speech Planner   page 2

5. OBJECTIONS: List likely objections and how you will answer them.

Objection   My Approach

6. SUPPORTING POINTS: Look at your brainstorm sheet, your main point, and your list of objections. Pick three or four major supporting points and list each one on a separate sheet of paper.

7. SUPPORT: Take the sheet for your first supporting point. List all the examples, statistics, anecdotes, analogies, explanations, and other supporting elements you might use. Do the same for the other supporting points.

8. OUTLINE: Select from your worksheets those points you wish to use in the speech. Put the points in logical order and construct a concise outline of the body of your speech.

9. OPENING: Write an opening which will catch the attention of the audience and show why the topic is relevant to them.

10. CLOSING: Write a closing which will tie up the presentation and leave your main point clear in the audience's mind.

Appendix IV

Types of Visual Equipment

Researchers have demonstrated what many good speakers already knew: audience retention goes up dramatically when good visual aids are added to a presentation. The power visual aids have is derived from several rather obvious effects. Good visual aids will:

1. Reinforce what the speaker says.

2. Focus the audience's attention.

3. Provide a change of pace.

4. Show things visually which are hard to describe. In an accident report, showing a map of the accident site can save 15 minutes of tedious description.

In many businesses and government agencies, visual aids are so common that a speech which lacks them is thought to be odd.

Sometimes the speech situation will dictate the type of visual aid equipment you are to use. At other times, the choice will be yours. You may also be in a position to decide on or influence the purchase of new equipment. You need to understand the strengths and weaknesses of competing systems to avoid wasting money on equipment which is mechanically

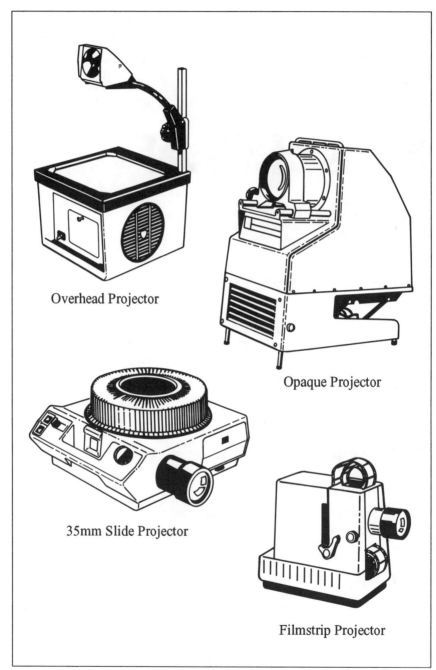

Figure A IV-1 - *Types of visual equipment.*

sound but unsuitable for the types of presentations actually given.

Since new types of visual aid equipment are invented every year, no printed list could be all-inclusive. This appendix describes a number of common types of visual aid equipment to help you make intelligent choices. Once you understand the principles involved in making these choices, you will be in a position to evaluate any new technology which might become available.

Overhead Projector

Because of its ease of use, the modern overhead transparency projector is standard equipment in many conference rooms and auditoriums. Most of the machines accept 8- by 10-inch transparencies, with or without a frame. The transparencies are sometimes called slides or (rarely) foils.

Overhead Advantages:

1. The projector can be used in a lighted room; however, it works better in subdued light.

2. The speaker can face the audience while operating the machine, making eye contact easy.

3. The order of slides can be easily changed, even during the speech itself. If the speaker is talking about slide 10 when the decision-maker asks about slide 2, the speaker can easily and quickly pull slide 2 out of the discard stack. With a 35mm projector and a remote, the speaker would have to reverse the machine and cycle back through slides 9 through 3.

4. The slides are large enough to be previewed without using a projector. Speakers can also integrate visual aid handling into a rehearsal without having a projector.

5. The speaker can pencil speech notes on the slide frames and cover sheets.

6. The transparencies are easy to make by a variety of methods. Lead time is typically short. A speaker equipped with a pair of scissors, a roll of double-stick tape or a bottle of rubber cement, and a box of transparencies can use a hotel copy machine to turn this morning's newspaper headlines into transparencies.

6. An impromptu visual aid can be made during the speech by writing on a blank transparency with a transparency marker (a special felt-tip pen). While printing on the overhead, the speaker can face the audience.

7. The equipment is relatively inexpensive with some units sale-priced below $200.

8. Slides are light and easy to transport.

9. Light, portable projectors are available, but often unnecessary because the system is so common.

10. Mechanical problems are uncommon. The only common problem is play in the vertical arm, which is caused by repeatedly carrying the unit by the vertical arm instead of supporting the base.

11. Bulb changes are simple in all models and virtually instantaneous in most.

Overhead Disadvantages:

1. Someone must stay close to the projector to change slides.

2. The projected image can be hard to read at a distance. Overhead projectors can be bought with different focal length lenses and more powerful projection lamps, but the overhead models typically found in most facilities are suitable only for small- to medium-sized audiences.

3. It is difficult to position the projector and the speaker to allow all audience members an unobstructed view of the screen.

Recommendations:

If available, an overhead should normally be your first choice. Use other media only when you can identify a clear advantage.

Be prepared to make adjustments if you work outside your own country. American projectors are designed around transparencies the same size as 8½" by 11" paper. Projectors in the UK, Australia, and New Zealand are designed around transparencies the same size as A4 paper, which is longer and narrower.

35mm Slide Projector/Filmstrip Projector

Like the overhead projector, a 35mm slide projector is found in meeting rooms around the globe. It also shares many of the overhead's strengths and weaknesses. A filmstrip projector is a smaller (and much cheaper) cousin of the slide projector. The images thrown on the screen by the two machines are virtually identical because they project from the same type of film. A filmstrip is simply a roll or partial roll of developed 35mm slide film. Rather than being cut apart to make individual slides, the filmstrip is left intact and advanced through the projector one frame at a time.

35mm Advantages:

1. Both types of 35mm have more impact than an overhead. The difference is due to the higher contrast and color saturation typical of 35mm.

2. A 35mm slide projector is suitable for a larger audience than an overhead. (Not true of filmstrips; the projectors are typically low-powered.) The images you see on the screen of a movie theater are projected from 35mm film.

3. A 35mm slide projector may be operated remotely, which gives the speaker freedom of movement. The remote control may be attached to the projector by a long electric cable (cord) or it may be cordless.

4. Slides (or filmstrips) and projector are easy to transport.

5. Camera shots are easy to create with 35mm equipment and essential for documentary displays (the exact position of the boxcar after the derailment). Camera shots can also be projected on an overhead projector, but not so easily. To work on an overhead, camera film (typically 35mm) must be converted to 4" by 5" transparencies, which are inserted in a special attachment to the overhead projector. The conversion can be expensive, and most facilities do not have the projector attachments.

35mm Disadvantages:

1. Film processing requires a long lead time (typically a week) unless

you can do it in-house. Forget about making a slide from the morning headlines.

2. Mistakes in shooting will not be obvious until after processing. One mistake can double the time it takes to have a usable slide show.

3. One bad frame will ruin a filmstrip (but not slides).

4. When the slides are projected, the room must be darkened, which may not be possible. A half-dark room will keep the audience from seeing the speaker or the slides clearly.

5. If the room is dark enough for the screen, the speaker's notes will require supplemental light.

6. Eye contact is impossible.

7. The audience may go to sleep in the dark.

8. The audience cannot take notes.

9. Almost all the audience's attention will be on the screen, very little on the speaker.

10. On a filmstrip, the order of frames cannot be changed. With a slide carousel, the order of slides is difficult to change compared to overhead slides. Quick changes may result in slides upside down or reversed.

11. Since 35mm slide projectors are inherently more complicated than overhead projectors, they are more prone to breakdown. Remote control units are especially troublesome.

35mm Recommendations:

Use if you have access to a darkened room, at least a week's lead time, and at least one of the following conditions:

1. An overhead is not available.

2. You need more impact than an overhead provides.

3. You need documentary pictures.

4. Your audience is too large for an overhead.

5. You need the freedom of remote control.

Flip Chart/Flip Cards

Most of us are familiar with the flip chart, a pad of paper (small to giant-sized) which is flipped one sheet at a time. A flip card system is similar, but uses a stack of poster board cards.

Flip Chart/Cards Advantages:

1. No electricity required. Ideal for National Guard maneuvers or a briefing at a construction site. Useful in other places.

2. Cheap. No equipment required (although an easel is a convenience).

3. The speaker can pencil notes on each sheet.

4. Easy to use impromptu. (If you request audience inputs, someone can write them on a blank sheet as they are called out.)

5. Short lead time to produce. Can be created with little notice.

Flip Chart/Cards Disadvantages:

1. Cannot be enlarged. Suitable only for small audiences.

2. The supporting easels are notorious for collapsing.

3. Pages flip in the wind.

4. One wrong letter requires redrawing an entire page.

5. Difficult to letter neatly. Most people find it easier to letter overhead transparencies because the size of letters is closer to normal writing.

6. Short speakers working with a standard-sized easel have trouble flipping the pages. Flip cards are easier, though.

7. The speaker cannot maintain eye contact while printing or drawing on the chart.

8. Large charts are extremely awkward to transport.

9. Look less professional than other media.

Recommendations:

Use only with small audiences. Use when electricity or better equipment is not available.

Chalkboard/Whiteboard

Chalkboards come in black or green. Whiteboards come in white. Chalkboards have been used for centuries; whiteboards are a new invention. Whiteboards are sold in various sizes under various trade names. The basic unit consists of a metal sheet covered with porcelain, formica, or plastic. The user can move magnetized objects on the board, or write on it with special erasable felt-tip pens.

Chalkboard/Whiteboard Advantages:

1. Chalkboards are very common.

2. Easy to improvise with.

3. No mechanical problems.

4. Very low operating costs (chalk & markers).

Chalkboard/Whiteboard Disadvantages:

1. Chalk dust!

2. Speaker must break eye contact to use the board, a severe disadvantage if very much writing is done.

3. Difficult to letter neatly. Most people find it easier to letter overhead transparencies because the size of letters is closer to normal writing.

4. Spelling errors are common.

5. Chalkboards are difficult to read and have little impact. Whiteboards are better.

Recommendations:

1. You may improvise on a board in response to a question if you can do it quickly. Otherwise, the audience will go to sleep looking at your back.

2. Other uses should be avoided.

3. If you have no choice but to put a lot of information on the board, write it on the board before your speech and uncover it at the appropriate time. Always choose a white-board over a chalkboard.

Samples/Models/Pictures

Samples, models, and pictures represent a unique class of visual aids. When appropriate, they can make a presentation more dramatic, but their applicability is limited. Basically, they should be considered supplements to other types of visual aids.

A sample is a concrete example of the thing being discussed. A product manager briefing the staff on the new breakfast cereal package would be expected to bring along a sample package. A police officer briefing parents on warning signs of drug abuse would likely bring along samples of drug paraphernalia.

A model is an object which looks like the real thing but isn't. A dentist talking to children about brushing techniques is likely to use a larger than life model of human teeth.

A picture is typically used when a sample or model would be impractical.

Samples/Models/Pictures Advantages:

1. Samples give a vivid sense of reality. ("This simple brass fitting, which you can hold in your hand, cost the Air Force $362.) Quoting from a book is more dramatic and more believable if you bring the book and read from it.

2. Models can show things which are not otherwise visible, i.e. a clear plastic auto engine block, which shows the moving parts.

3. Models and samples hold attention well.

Samples/Models/Pictures Disadvantages:

1. Some models are costly to build.

2. Some models, samples, and pictures are too small to be seen clearly by the audience.

3. Objects passed among audience members will distract attention from the speaker.

Recommendation:

Use whenever possible to supplement other visual aids. Rarely does anything else convey an equal sense of reality.

Conventional Movies

All the jokes and griping you have heard about boring training films should alert you to possible problems. A short film clip which is well made can add greatly to a presentation's success. The same presentation can be destroyed by a poorly made or mishandled film.

Movie Advantages:

1. Can be highly dramatic with great impact.

2. Can provide documentary evidence.

3. Suitable for very large audiences.

Movie Disadvantages:

1. Noisy projector.

2. Requires dark room. Speaker needs supplemental light to read notes.

3. Camera, projector, and processing are all expensive. You can buy a VHS tape with up to six hours of recording time on sale for less than you would have spent in 1972 to have a five-minute roll of 8mm movie film developed.

4. Very long lead time to produce.

5. Difficult to produce high quality product without professional help.

6. Difficult to change.

7. Many people have forgotten how to run the projectors.

8. Projectors are prone to mechanical problems.

9. Speaker cannot control or change the pace of the presentation.

Recommendations:

1. Use only as a supplement to provide documentation or increase impact.

2. Show the shortest segment which will accomplish your purpose.

3. Consider existing films first. Convert existing films to videotape unless you need extremely high impact.

4. Make a new film only if lots of money and expertise are available.

Videotapes

Although the technology is radically different, a videotape and conventional movie have about the same relation to a speech. Each of them should only supplement other visual aids.

Video Advantages:

1. Impact is considerable, though less than a conventional movie's.

2. Videotape itself is ultra-cheap compared to conventional movie film.

3. Does not require a completely dark room.

4. Equipment is quite common and many people know how to operate it.

5. Tapes are easy to transport.

6. Compared to conventional movies, lead time is very short (tape can be used immediately after shooting).

Video Disadvantages:

1. Speaker cannot control or change the pace of the presentation.

2. Video cassette recorder and camera are expensive.

3. Picture quality on older units is noticeably poorer than with conventional movies.

4. Difficult to use with large audiences. With large audiences, use multiple TVs or a video projector (both expensive options).

5. Various formats are incompatible.

Recommendations:

1. Use to supplement other visual aids when greater impact or documentary evidence is needed.

2. Choose video over conventional movies unless a large audience must watch.

Opaque Projector

Imagine how convenient it would be if you never had to make a slide, if you could simply insert a sheet of paper, or a book, or a picture into a machine and have that image projected for your audience. That dream come true is the promise of an opaque projector. However, the side effects can make the dream into a nightmare.

A graphics shop can make good use of an opaque projector by projecting a diagram in a book onto a wall, where it can guide an artist making a poster. The machines are much less useful for speakers.

Opaque Projector Advantages:

1. No need to convert anything into another media.

2. No lead time.

3. High quality projection of pictures.

Opaque Projector Disadvantages:

1. Room must be *totally* dark.

2. Older machines are heavy and bulky.

3. The machine gets extremely hot while operating. I have scorched a photograph while attempting to project it.

4. Changing from one image to another is time-consuming.

Recommendation:

Don't even consider it!

LCD Panel/PC Projector

Basically an accessory for an overhead projector, an LCD panel, also known as a PC projector, allows you to project anything which appears on your computer monitor onto a large screen. The equipment itself is a shallow box (typically 12" by 13" by 2") with glass on the top and bottom and metal or plastic on the sides. A computer cable is attached, and sometimes a power cord, as well. The products are sometimes known by their brand names, such as MagnaByte from Telex, DATASHOW from Kodak, and the Computer Projection Panel from Sharp.

The gadget functions like a rather fat, infinitely variable overhead transparency. Once the LCD panel is hooked to your computer, the letters and other images of your computer screen are reproduced inside the box where they can be projected by the overhead.

Most models have remote controls, and some have wireless remotes. High tech one-upsmanship should make LCD panels very popular in the near future.

LCD Panel Advantages:

1. Ideal for demonstrating computer programs. Think about the difference between having 60 people crowd around one computer screen and having them sitting in chairs watching an 8' by 8' screen.

2. No misaligned slides.

3. Limited animation possible (if the computer supports it).

4. Allows quick switches between images (if the computer is quick).

5. The projector and computer can be separated to prevent the speaker from blocking the audience's view.

6. Short lead time. As soon as you can type it on the computer, you have an image ready to project.

7. Easily portable (if the computer and projector are portable or available on site). Weight is about six pounds. If the facility you are going to has a computer, overhead projector, and LCD panel, you need oniy bring a floppy disk.

LCD Panel Disadvantages:

1. Color models are expensive – but the price is slowly dropping.

2. Low contrast can make images hard to see. Angle of vision is critical; people sitting on the sides when the screen is in the front of the room will have a hard time.

3. Audiences can be distracted by the gyrations some computers go through to update the screen.

Recommendations:

1. If you are demonstrating a computer program, use it.

2. Test any unit you are considering in the room where you will use it to see if the low contrast and angle of vision concerns are tolerable.

Multi-Media

Several years ago, *multi-media presentation* was a buzzword among business and professional groups. A certain mystique seemed to surround anyone who could integrate several slide projectors and a movie projector into a single show. Some of the glamour has faded now, but there is still a feeling in some quarters that a presentation with two projectors is inherently better than a presentation with only one.

In considering whether to go multi-media, you should consider several factors. If a multi-media show is well planned and well synchronized, the results are impressive. But if anything goes wrong, the results are awful. Unless you are trying to market your services as a multi-media producer, the success of a presentation will not be measured by its slickness.

Normally, you should choose the type(s) of visual aids which let you make your points most effectively. If you can make all your points with 35mm slides, don't bother dragging in a TV set and VCR. It will only add to your rehearsal time and increase the risk of equipment failure.

Simple visual aids with a professional appearance are usually best.

Appendix V
Conference Presentation Guide

    Appendix V contains Master Copies of the Conference Presentation Guide which can be copied as often as necessary without the author's permission.

Conference Presentation Guide

This Guide was designed for use by people with academic, business, professional, or government backgrounds when they are on the program at a conference or convention. The Guide works equally well for individual presenters and panel members. The steps are also useful in planning presentations for other contexts.

Most conferences are planned by a program committee, which may invite experts to participate or may solicit program proposals or research papers/reports. The committee may combine several proposals or papers on similar subjects to form a panel session. After the program committee accepts a program proposal or paper, the presenter typically has several responsibilities:

1. To prepare a written description of the session for the advance conference schedule.

2. To prepare the final paper for publication in the conference notes or proceedings.

3. To prepare and polish an oral presentation for delivery at the conference.

This appendix offers a concise description of the essential steps in preparing and delivering the conference presentation. The inexperienced speaker can use it as a guide through unfamiliar territory while the experienced speaker will find it helpful as a checklist to ensure nothing is forgotten. Either way, the pages should be copied, so actions can be checked off as they are done.

Upon Notification . . .

Scope

☐ Determine the scope of your presentation.

 ☐ How long is the session?

 ☐ Who else will speak at the same session?

 ☐ Should presenters' topics be adjusted to avoid overlap?

 ☐ How long should your presentation be? How much time should you allow for questions?

 ☐ Will questions be taken during each presentation, at the end of each presentation, or at the end of all presentations?

☐ What equipment will be available?

NOTE: The session moderator and program chair are the best sources for information about the session and about the other panel members.

Outline

☐ Convert your proposal or paper into a presentation outline using the steps below.

NOTE: At most conferences, you will not be allowed to simply read your paper. The audience can do that for themselves. The conference presentation should highlight key points and allow interaction with the audience. Most successful presenters talk from an outline written on paper or index cards. You may, of course, memorize the outline, but memorizing the entire presentation word for word will make it sound stale.

 ☐ Select the most important points from your paper or other sources. In most cases you will have more material than you can cover in the allotted time. You should attempt to cover a few points well rather than many points hastily.

 ☐ Choose a central theme. The presentation will lack unity unless every point can be related to the theme. Your theme or objective must be simple enough to state in one fairly short sentence. It should answer the question: "What is the one thing I want my audience to know or do after my presentation?"

NOTE: The theme of your presentation need not be the same as the theme of your paper. (The audience can always read your paper in the conference notes or proceedings.)

☐ Develop interesting practical examples to support your subpoints.

☐ Sketch possible visual aids.

☐ Organize your points into a logical pattern.

☐ Develop a strong opening which will arrest the audience's attention and provide a clear road map for the rest of the presentation.

☐ Create a conclusion which will cement your main point and provide an air of finality.

Visual Aids

☐ Select a medium for your visual aids.

NOTE: Flip charts are normally too small for a conference setting. Movies and videotapes are difficult to integrate and should be used only if they are unavoidable. Overhead projector transparencies and 35mm slides work well. The 35mm format is easier to read when projected and provides more impact, but the overhead projector allows you to work with some of the lights on, making it easier for you to see the audience and your notes.

☐ Prepare your visual aids.

NOTE: If you are a teacher, remember that typical conference conditions are likely to be worse than the classroom conditions with which you are familiar. Slides which can be read at 25 feet in a darkened classroom may be invisible at 65 feet in a brighter room.

☐ Make only one point with each slide.

☐ Simplify graphic designs.

☐ Limit each slide to six lines of six words each.

☐ Use the largest possible lettering.

☐ Make every graphics line and every letter as bold as possible.

NOTE: If your slides cannot be simplified to this extent, consider using another medium, such as a printed handout.

Rehearsal and Revision

☐ Rehearse the presentation. Most problems in delivery can be traced to inadequate rehearsal time or inappropriate rehearsal conditions. Effective rehearsals require maximum simulation. As far as possible you should rehearse:

    ☐ Out loud at full volume.

    ☐ In the same size room as the one where the presentation is scheduled.

    ☐ While manipulating all of your visual aids. (Strive to continue talking while you handle the slides.)

    ☐ In front of a live audience. (Station audience members at the extreme corners of the room.)

    ☐ While being videotaped, if possible.

NOTE: You may have difficulty arranging maximum simulation for all rehearsals, but you should attempt to have as many rehearsals as possible under conditions similar to the conference. To rehearse merely by repeating the presentation silently to yourself is to court disaster in the physical aspects of delivery.

NOTE: If you are a teacher, remember that a polished, professional conference presentation will require considerably more practice than a normal classroom lecture.

☐ Poll your rehearsal audience.

    ☐ Could each of them hear you clearly?

    ☐ Were the visual aids easy to read from the farthest point?

☐ Was the point of each visual aid obvious?

☐ Did you handle the visual aids smoothly?

☐ Was your overall organization clear?

☐ Were any of your points unclear?

☐ Did you have any distracting mannerisms? (Jingling coins? Tugging at skirt? Playing with pointer? Pacing? Other?)

☐ Was the pace too fast to follow easily?

☐ Was the pace too slow to be interesting?

☐ Did you maintain eye contact?

☐ Did you run overtime?

☐ Revise the presentation based on audience input. If the pace of your delivery was successful, but you ran overtime, cut material rather than speeding up.

☐ Select a portion of the presentation near the end which you can take out or leave in depending on how long the presentation is running.

☐ Repeat rehearsals to polish the presentation and gain confidence.

At the Conference . . .

When You Arrive

☐ Contact your panel moderator and the other panelists to arrange a pre-session meeting.

☐ Keep checking at the conference desk for last minute changes to the time or place for your session.

At the Pre-Session Meeting

☐ Review decisions about order of presenters, time limits, and handling of questions.

☐ Arrange a timing signal to indicate how much of your time is left.

☐ Give a copy of your typed introduction to the session moderator.

☐ Inspect the room.

    ☐ Determine placement of equipment. Putting the screen in a corner usually provides better sightlines for the audience.

    ☐ Check the audience seating. Chairs in bad locations should be removed or roped off.

    ☐ Decide where each presenter will sit.

    ☐ Check the route from your seat to the podium. Are there cords to trip on? Loose steps beside the platform? Chairs, tables, or equipment in the way?

    ☐ Test the equipment. How does it operate? Are there spare bulbs? Do you need the mike? Who will dim the lights?

    ☐ Try your slides. Can they be seen? If someone else will be flipping your slides, arrange signals.

Ten Minutes Before the Session

☐ Find the room monitor or room manager and introduce yourself.

☐ Ask someone in the back row to signal if you cannot be heard clearly.

☐ Re-check equipment placement and operation.

☐ Check the order of your slides.

☐ Find your seat. Review the hazards between you and the podium. If time remains, you may want to chat with members of the audience.

During Your Presentation

☐ Take several deep breaths just before you walk to the podium.

☐ Do not start talking the instant you reach the podium. Take a moment to collect yourself and look at the audience. Remember to smile.

☐ Deliver the presentation as you rehearsed it.

☐ Do not panic at mistakes. Audiences expect an occasional slip of the tongue. Simply correct yourself and go on. If you miss a slide, forget it; the audience will never know.

Handling Questions

☐ Take questions from different parts of the room.

☐ Repeat each question. Use paraphrasing to focus the unfocused question and soften the hostile question.

☐ Defer your answer until the break if a question concerns only one person or is off the subject.

☐ Direct your answers to the entire audience.

☐ Avoid belittling or condescending answers.

☐ Be ready to cut off questions because of time.

After the Session

☐ Collect your material to allow the next group to set up.

☐ Move to the hallway to answer additional questions and talk with audience members.

☐ Thank the room manager.

☐ Report problems or suggestions to the program committee or conference director.

☐ Rest.

Recommended Resources

Books and Articles

Berkman, Robert I. *Find It Fast: How to Uncover Expert Information on Any Subject.* New York: Harper & Row, 1990.

The Bully Pulpit: Quotations From America's Presidents. Elizabeth Frost, ed. New York: New England Publishing Associates, 1988.

Carter, Judy. *Stand-Up Comedy.* New York: Dell, 1989.

de Mare, George. *Communicating at the Top.* New York: John Wiley & Sons, 1979.

Dormann, Henry O. *The Speaker's Book of Quotations.* New York: Fawcett Columbine, 1987.

Harlan, Raymond C. and Walter M. Woolfson, Jr. *Telemarketing That Works: How To Create A Winning Program For Your Company.* Chicago: Probus, 1991.

Harris, Sherwood. *The New York Public Library Book of How and Where to Look it Up.* New York: Prentice Hall, 1991.

Humes, James C. *Podium Humor: A Raconteur's Treasure of Witty and Humorous Stories.* New York: Harper & Row, 1975.

Huseman, Richard C., et al. *Business Communication: Strategies and Skills,* 2nd edition. Chicago: Dryden Press, 1985.

Iapoce, Michael. *A Funny Thing Happened on the Way to the Boardroom.* New York: John Wiley and Sons, 1988.

Kirkpatrick, Donald L. *How To Plan And Conduct Productive Business Meetings.* Chicago: Dartnell, 1976.

Lieberman, Gerald F. *3,500 Good Quotes for Speakers.* Garden City, NY: Doubleday, 1983.

The Linton Trainer's Resource Directory, 2nd ed. Hopkins, MN: Linton Publishing, 1992.

Lorayne, Harry. *How To Develop a Super-Power Memory.* New York: NAL Penguin, 1985.

Mager, Robert. *The New Mager Library* (2nd ed.). Belmont, CA: David S. Lake Publishers, 1984.

McFarland, Kenneth. *Eloquence in Public Speaking.* Englewood Cliffs, NJ: Prentice-Hall, 1961.

Murphy, Herta A. and Herbert W. Hildebrandt. *Effective Business Communications,* 4th edition. New York: McGraw-Hill, 1984.

Walters, Dottie. *Speak and Grow Rich.* Englewood Cliffs, NJ: Prentice-Hall, 1990.

Wills, Garry. "The Words That Remade America: Lincoln at Gettysburg," *The Atlantic,* June 1992.

Audio Tape Sets

Canfield, Jack. *How To Build High Self Esteem.* Chicago: Nightingale-Conant.

D'Arcy, Jan. *Speak Without Fear.* Chicago: Nightingale-Conant.

Fleming, Carol. *The Sound of Your Voice.* Chicago: Nightingale-Conant.

Qubein, Nido. *How To Be a Great Communicator.* Chicago: Nightingale-Conant.

Trudeau, Kevin. *Mega Memory.* Chicago: Nightingale-Conant.

Training Information Services
(Discussed in Chapter 23)

Seminar Clearinghouse International. P.O. Box 1757, St. Paul, MN 55101-0757.

Seminar Information Service. 17752 Skypark Circle, Suite 210, Irvine, CA 92714. 714/261-9104. Fax: 714/261-1963.

Timeplace, Inc. 460 Totten Pond Road, Waltham, MA 02154. 617/890-4636.

Other Services and Associations

American Society For Training and Development. 1640 King Street, Box 1443, Alexandria, VA 22313-2043. 703/683-8100. Fax: 703/683-8103. Discussed in Chapter 23.

Culturgrams [sic]. Publication Services branch of the David M. Kennedy Center for International Studies at Brigham Young University. Mailing address: 280 HRCB, Provo, UT 84602. 801/378-6528. A good quick source for information on cultural expectations in other countries.

Current Comedy. 700 Orange St., P.O. Box 1992, Wilmington, DE 19801. Phone 800-777-7098. A service offering original material you can use.

International Association of Business Communicators. One Hallidie Plaza, Suite 600, San Francisco, CA 94102. 415/433-3400. Fax 415/362-8762. Areas of interest include internal communication, external communication, marketing, electronic communication, executive-level communication management, and mid-level communication management.

National Speakers Association. 1500 South Priest Drive, Tempe, AZ 85281. 602/968-2552. Fax: 602/968-0911. Discussed in Chapter 23.

The Speech Communication Association. 5105 Backlick Road, Building E, Annandale, VA 22003. 703/750-0533. Fax: 703/914-9471. Focus on research and academic teaching. Source of useful information about speaking and training.

Walters Speaker Services. P.O. Box 1120, Glendora, CA 91740. 818/335-8069. FAX: 818/335-6127. Discussed in Chapter 23.

References

(1) *The Book of Lists,* ed. by David Wallechinsky, et al, New York: William Morrow and Co., 1977, pp. 469-470.

(2) Bill Osher and Sioux Henley Campbell, *The Blue Chip Graduate,* Atlanta: Peachtree Publishers, 1987, pp. 21-22.

(3) Virginia Culver, "Graham, stage fright old chums," *The Denver Post,* 12 Jul 87, p. 1-A.

(4) Cicero, *De Oratore,* p. XXVI.

(5) Alan Rozanski, et al, "Mental Stress and the Induction of Silent Myocardial Ischemia in Patients with Coronary Artery Disease," *The New England Journal of Medicine,* Vol. 318, No. 16, 21 Apr 88, pp. 1005-1011.

(6) Reporting on a number of studies, Michael J. Beatty wrote, "In general, these studies suggest that most speakers experience considerable arousal during public speaking whether or not they are fearful. However this arousal engenders pressure to understand and label the sensation. It is how an individual labels this arousal that determines the emotion experienced. Accordingly, a person who perceives himself or herself to be a poor speaker would interpret increased heart rate during public speaking as fear or anxiety whereas a confident speaker might view the arousal as excitement and requisite to *vigorous and effective speech.*" Michael J. Beatty, "Situational and Predispositional Correlates of Public Speaking Anxiety," *Communication Education,* Vol. 37, No. 1, Jan 88, p. 29.

(7) Culver, p. 1-A.

(8) Beatty, p. 37.

(9) Aristotle, *Rhetoric*, 2.1. 1377b-1378a.

(10) Ibid.

(11) My exposure to the idea originally came from Dart Peterson in a presentation he gave for the Southwest Ohio Chapter of the Society for Technical Communication.

(12) Quoted by Henry O. Dormann in *The Speaker's Book of Quotations*. New York: Fawcett Columbine, 1987, p. 105.

(13) Quoted by Henry O. Dormann in *The Speaker's Book of Quotations*. New York: Fawcett Columbine, 1987, p. 26.

(14) Quoted by Gerald F. Lieberman in *3,500 Good Quotes for Speakers*. Garden City, NY: Doubleday, 1983, p. 153.

(15) Abraham Lincoln, "Speech to the Young Men's Lyceum," (1838). Reprinted in Garry Wills, "The Words That Remade America: Lincoln at Gettysburg," *The Atlantic*, June 1992, p. 72. In this short article, Wills does an exceptional job of analyzing one of the most powerful speeches in the English language.

(16) James C. Humes, *Podium Humor: A Raconteur's Treasury of Witty and Humorous Stories*, New York: Harper & Row, 1975.

(17) Humes, p. 167.

(18) Humes, p. 197.

(19) "Some Answers No One Expected," *New York Times*, 8 April 1987.

(20) "Campanis wants his troubles to bring changes," *Dayton Daily News and Journal Herald*, 4 July 1987, p. 10.

(21) "Campanis Is Out; Racial Remarks Cited by Dodgers," *New York Times*, 9 April 1987, p. B13.

(22) William Shakespeare, 1 Henry IV, V, iv, 119-120.

(23) George de Mare, *Communicating at the Top*, New York: John Wiley & Sons, 1979, pp. 108-110.

(24) Headline in Topeka, Kansas, *Capital-Journal,* reprinted in *Reader's Digest*, Dec 1991, p. 57.

(25) Anyone wishing to explore these ideas in more depth should consult the five short easy-to-read books in *The New Mager Library*, by Robert Mager (2nd ed.), Belmont, CA: David S. Lake Publishers, 1984.

(26) Most of these ideas are taken from Joan Gorham, ''The Relationship Between Verbal Teacher Immediacy Behaviors and Student Learning,'' *Communication Education*, Vol. 37, No. 1 (Jan 88), pp. 40-53.

Index

G

gathering evidence, 42
gestures while speaking, 133
good news/bad news, 77
Graham, Billy, 3, 5

H

hand-held microphone, 138
hard sell approach, 57
Harlan, Ross, 42, 204
harnessing nervous energy, 8
herringbone room arrangement, 125
Hippenmeyer, Bill, 38
history of organization, 28-31
hoarseness, remedy for, 137
hobbies, using as subject, 202
honesty of speaker, 14
HOP, 206-207
Hope, Bob, 67
horseshoe room arrangement, 123,
    124
hostile questions, 161-162
Humes, James C., 75
humor
    importance of good taste, 64-
        66
    self-deprecating, 75
    use of, 63, 203-205, 207
    vs. serious issues, 66
hypothetical stories, 72

I

impromptu speaking, 187-193
improving employee performance,
    210
incongruity, 203
index cards, 113
informal research, 43
informative
    after-dinner speech, 201
    speech, 11
inoculation, audience, 48

interactive sales approach, 196-197
International Training in Communi-
    cation, 173, 174
interviews, television, 177-186
introductions, 52, 215-218
inventing jokes, 76
irrelevant material, eliminating from
    introductions, 217

J

Jackson, Jesse, 60
J. C. Penney, 28
jokes
    adapting, 74
    inventing, 76
    testing, 67,
    use of, 41, 63-81

K

key-word outline, 113, 217
King, Martin Luther, Jr., 47, 55-56
Kissinger, Henry, 40
keystoning, 126

L

language
    appropriate, 130-132
    difficulties, 26
    linear nature of, 37
lapel-mounted microphone, 138
last-minute changes, 142-143
late-breaking curve pattern, 54
lavaliere microphone, 139
lazer printer, 94
LCD panel, 251-252
lecturing, 211-212
library research, 47
lighting, room, 150
Lincoln, Abraham, 60, 204
location, scouting of, 33, 34